THE :: :: HISTORICAL SAINT :: :: COLUMBA ::

THE WHITE PACK-HORSE BIDS FAREWELL TO THE DYING SAINT COLUMBA.

"*Ecce albus occurrit caballus, obediens servitor, qui scilicet lactaria bocetum inter et monasterium vascula gestare consueverat. Hic ad Sanctum accedens, mirum dictu, caput in sinu eius ponens, ut credo inspirante Deo, cui omne animal rerum sapit sensu quo iusserit ipse Creator, dominum a se suum mox emigraturum, et ipsum ultra non visurum sciens, coepit plangere, ubertimque, quasi homo, lacrymas in gremium Sancti fundere, et valde spumans flere.*"

THE HISTORICAL
SAINT COLUMBA

BY

W. DOUGLAS SIMPSON

M.A., D.LITT., F.S.A.SCOT.

LIBRARIAN IN THE UNIVERSITY OF ABERDEEN

(Second Edition)

SOME BOOKS ARE TO BE TASTED, OTHERS TO BE SWALLOWED,
AND SOME FEW TO BE CHEWED AND DIGESTED. — *Bacon*

PRINTERS AND PUBLISHERS

MILNE & HUTCHISON, ABERDEEN

1927

TO MY FRIEND

ALAN ORR ANDERSON

WITH

GRATEFUL APPRECIATION

OF HIS PATIENT LABOURS

IN EXPLORING AND SETTING FORTH

THE EARLY SOURCES OF SCOTTISH HISTORY

I DEDICATE THIS WORK

PREFACE.

AFTER the publication of my *Origins of Christianity in Aberdeenshire*—the germ of which was a lecture delivered before the Aberdeen Diocesan Association in October, 1924—I was invited, by the Committee of that body, in a subsequent lecture to express my view as to the real part played by St. Columba in the evangelisation of Scotland. This second lecture was duly delivered on 26th January, 1926: of it the present work is an expansion.

As the idea of St. Columba here presented is widely different from that hitherto in currency, it may be well that my thesis should be distinctly set forth at the outset. It has long seemed clear to me that the popular conception of St. Columba as the apostle of Scotland cannot sustain the test of rigid historical and archæological inquiry. The first condition of any adequate study of St. Columba's work must be a searching analysis of the political conditions of his epoch. Such an analysis reveals that Columba's countrymen, the Dalriadic Scots from Ireland, were bitterly hostile to the Picts into whose territory they had intruded. Throughout his career Columba comported himself, in my view, as a steady champion of the Scots, and I hold that his political activities were consistently directed against the Pictish King and people. Long before Columba's time, Christianity was already widely spread among the Picts, who had their own organised Church—between which and Columba, if my reading of the evidence be right, there was either active hostility or, at best, a complete absence of co-operation. I believe that the real scope of St. Columba's labours can be shown to have been almost entirely restricted to his fellow-nationals of Dalriada—the early Scotic kingdom corresponding roughly to Argyllshire—and to the Pictish tribes of the borderland; with an extension into Strathtay, and probably another extension along the Great Glen towards Inverness.

I have endeavoured to trace, step by step, the stages in the historic process by which the scope of Columba's influence became so hugely exaggerated in subsequent times; and I have illustrated, by an analysis of particular cases such as the famous "Myth of Deer," the way in which the name of Columba was linked with centres of early Pictish Christianity, to the detriment of the due renown of the real missionaries by whom the True Faith was first taught in regions far beyond Columba's purview.

Such a historical revision of Columba's place in Scottish origins is no new development. So far back as 1885 the late Dr. Alexander MacBain had some understanding of the facts, which moved him emphatically to record his conviction that Columba "swallowed up into his own fame all the work of his predecessors, companions, and contemporaries, and deprived generations of pioneers and missionaries of their just fame" (*Transactions of the Gaelic Society of Inverness,* Vol. XI., p. 150). And in 1894 Bishop John Dowden also sounded a warning note: "however great the fame of Columba justly is, other independent missionaries of monastic foundations distinct from his had their share in the work of evangelising Scotland" (*The Celtic Church in Scotland,* p. 121). More recently, the view that the radius of Columba's activities is much overstated has been maintained with great vigour and learning by the Rev. Archibald B. Scott, and is fully set forth by him in his thought-provoking work on *The Pictish Nation* (1918). There are many things in Mr. Scott's reading of our early history to which, like others, I cannot subscribe; and the value of his book is seriously impaired by the false view that he has unhappily adopted as to the Romano-Pictish frontier in the time of St. Ninian. But so far as Columba is concerned, I feel myself substantially in agreement with Mr. Scott's main position. Professed Celtic scholarship has earned little credit by the conspiracy of silence with which it has treated a work that—whether one agree with it or no—remains something to be reckoned with by every student of this difficult period.

To my great loss, Professor William J. Watson's *History of the Celtic Place-Names of Scotland* (1926) appeared too late for me to make full use of it. While recognising amply the high value of this fine work, I feel bound to draw attention to what seems to me a cardinal defect in its treatment of the subject. Although the author styles himself on the title page "Professor of Celtic Languages, Literature, History, and Antiquities," yet, in dealing with the many important and complex historical problems that it raises, his book has almost nothing whatever to say as to the archæological evidence. Indeed, I hold it a grave misfortune that the early Celtic period in Scottish history has hitherto been well-nigh exclusively a battle-ground of the linguists. Their capacity for sustained disagreement among themselves is so phenomenal that the archæologist is justified in raising his voice amid their clamour, in order to invite attention to a mass of vital evidence, the significance of which they have for the most part utterly ignored. The importance of this neglected avenue of research is fully set forth in the following pages. I have sought to show how the Pictish Church exhibits a series of monumental remains totally different, alike in origins and development, from those found in the region of Scotic influence west of Drumalban (the central mountain backbone of Scotland).

In a work where this line of evidence bulks so large, I am fortunate, through the generosity of the Council of the Society of Antiquaries of Scotland, in being able to illustrate my book to an extent which otherwise would have been impossible. The blocks for the following illustrations have been lent by the Council:—Figs. 7-12, 14-16, 18-25, 27, 29, 32, 33, 35, 46-61, 63, 66-68, 71-73, 75-77. The illustrations at Figs. 5 and 62 are reproduced from the Rev. E. C. Trenholme's *Story of Iona*, by kind permission of his representatives, and of the publishers, Messrs. Douglas & Foulis, Limited, Edinburgh. Those at Figs. 30, 31 and 78 are from the Right Rev. Bishop G. F. Browne's *Antiquities in the Neighbourhood of Dunecht*; and for permission to use them I am indebted to the author, to the Right Hon. the Viscount Cowdray, and to the Syndics of the Cambridge University Press. The map at Fig. 38 is reproduced, with some additions, by courtesy of the Royal Commission on the Ancient and Historical Monuments of Scotland. For the blocks of Figs. 39-44, I am indebted to Mr. C. R. Peers, C.B.E., H.M. Chief Inspector of Ancient Monuments, and to the Council of the Society of Antiquaries of London. Mr. Symington Grieve most readily allowed me to reproduce the photographs of the Oronsay Cross (Fig. 65) from his *Book of Colonsay and Oronsay*. The block for Fig. 70 was lent by Messrs. Jolly & Sons, Limited, Aberdeen. The map at Fig. 3 is completed from a survey begun in 1903 by Dr. Thomas Ross, who kindly gave me his unfinished draft. I owe to Mr. Leslie G. Thomson the photograph at Fig. 4. The other illustrations are from blocks already in my own possession, or specially made for the present work.

Besides elucidating my argument from the archæological evidence, the series of illustrations which I have thus been able to collect will also, I hope, reveal to the general reader how rich and splendid is the artistic heritage that still remains to us, despite the waste of ages, from the Celtic period of our country's history.

By arrangement with the artist, I am privileged to reproduce, as my Frontispiece, the beautiful painting of Columba saying farewell to the pack-horse, by Mr. John Duncan, R.S.A.

And, finally, I must record my deep appreciation of the vigilant care which my publishers have bestowed upon every aspect of the production of a book demanding more than usual exactness in the printing of its numerous footnotes and references.

The writing of the present work has inevitably involved traversing anew much of the ground already covered in my *Origins of Christianity in Aberdeenshire*. Where this has been necessary, I have preferred simply to repeat the language of the former treatise, rather than to indulge myself in what John Richard Green has called "the affectation of re-writing such a passage for the mere sake of giving it an air of novelty.''

It would be ungenerous not to take this opportunity of expressing my high sense of the manner in which my previous little work has been received, even by those not prepared to accept its conclusions. It gives me great pleasure to record my gratitude to the various correspondents who have favoured me with corrections and additional information, particularly in regard to questions of local topography and antiquities. Through the kind co-operation of these willing helpers, the task of converting what was merely a provisional statement into a really adequate account of the origins of Christianity in north-eastern Scotland has been made much easier.

I cannot better conclude this Preface than by quoting a passage from the writings of Dr. George Petrie, the distinguished Celtic archæologist. ''I am sensitively aware that I am running the greatest danger of being deemed rash and visionary. But confiding, as I do, in the honesty of my purpose, which is solely to inquire after truth in a spirit of candour, such an anticipation presents to me no terrors; and I feel confident that those best qualified to judge of the difficulties of my undertaking will not censure the expression of opinions, however novel, which are offered for consideration in such a spirit, and which, even if erroneous, being based on evidences which I submit to be tested by the learned, must equally tend to the discovery of truth, as if they had themselves been incontrovertible.''

W. DOUGLAS SIMPSON.

KING'S COLLEGE,
    UNIVERSITY OF ABERDEEN,
        March, 1927.

PREFACE TO THE SECOND EDITION.

As the type of the first edition was kept standing, it has not been possible to do more than make necessary corrections in the body of the book.   But in the *Addenda* I have incorporated some fresh information, and have sought to meet sundry criticisms; while in the Introduction I have outlined my conception of that general background of the Christian penetration of Scotland against which I would seek to portray Columba's career; and have also endeavoured to justify my estimate of his personality.   I am particularly happy to use this opportunity of expressing my deep sense of gratitude to the numerous critics and correspondents in this country, in Ireland, and on the Continent, who have kindly favoured me with notes of corrections and fresh material.   I hope it will be understood that only considerations of space have prevented me in many cases from utilising so much additional matter.

It should have been stated in the first Preface that the chronology followed throughout the book is that worked out by Mr. A. O. Anderson in his *Early Sources of Scottish History*.

W. D. S.

November, 1927.

CONTENTS.

INTRODUCTION TO THE SECOND EDITION.

IT is astonishing how little systematic work has yet been done towards identifying and working out what may be described as the penetration lines of Christianity in Scotland. The history of Christian origins in the land then known as Alba has too long been presented merely as an unrelated series of pretty legends, dealing more or less mythically with the lives of individual saints. Until recently no real effort has been made to grapple with the problem, basically and scientifically, by the correlation of historical, topographical, and archæological evidence with the germs of ancient truth still lurking in the medieval lives of the early missionaries. The facts of the case have also been obscured by the overgrown reputation of St. Columba, to whom it has long been customary to ascribe almost the entire Christianisation of Pictland— an estimate which ignores the work of many an eminent Britonic or Pictish evangelist, who lived before or after Columba, and worked independently of him and his Scotic Church of Iona.

It cannot be too distinctly understood that the early missionaries, whencesoever they came, could not and did not roam over the country at haphazard. Their activities were conditioned by geography and by political arrangements; and problems also of communications and supply had to be kept constantly in view.

Clearly, therefore, any rational attempt to understand the evangelisation of Scotland must take into account the permanent geographical conditions of the country. All through its history two dominating features have asserted their influence in determining the course alike of military, political, and ecclesiastical events. The first and by far the more important of these features is the great mountain backbone known as Drumalban, the *Dorsum Britanniae* of Adamnan and other early writers—the central watershed of Alba, running northwards from Ben Lomond to Ben Hope. All through the past of Scotland, from remotest prehistoric times, this majestic barrier of splintered ben and wine-dark moorland has been a dividing line no less cultural than political. The second dominant feature is the transverse line

xv

known as the Mounth, the upland ridge flanking the southern bank of the Dee, between Girdleness and Lochnagar (properly called the White Mounth). Although its influence on medieval strategy and local administrative arrangements was considerable, the Mounth seems never to have been a political and still less a cultural barrier of major importance at any period in Scottish history. It is often stated to have formed the boundary between the northern and the southern Picts, but this is quite an unwarranted inference; and in any case it is more than doubtful whether the division into northern and southern Picts, as used by Bede,[1] connoted anything more than a convenient geographical expression. No clear evidence of a political division along any such line can be found in the later period of Pictish history. At all events, the reason for the comparative unimportance of the Mounth barrier is apparent on a glance at the map. While its west end is securely buttressed by the great central *massif* of the Grampians, its eastern termination on the North Sea lies open, and is capable of being turned from the central Scottish plain *via* Strathmore and the Cairnamounth, Slug Mounth and Causey Mounth passes. Along these lines, accordingly, the northern districts of Scotland have always been pierced by invading armies, from Roman times onwards. The approach to the central plain is easier and quicker from the west, from Carlisle (the Roman *Luguvallium*) *via* Annandale and Clydesdale; or from the centre by Melrose (*Trimontium*, the great fort at Newstead) and Lauderdale to Channelkirk and Inveresk; than from the east over the long bleak inhospitable Berwickshire moors. Both the western and the central routes were used by Agricola in his various campaigns, A.D. 80-84; but the central route was the more in favour of the two, and it was only in the Antonine period, after the building of the northern wall (A.D. 143) that the Annandale and Clydesdale highway was occupied in force, and became of great importance as the approach to the western end of the wall.[2] In 208-11 the Emperor Severus adopted the eastward access, but outflanked the Berwickshire moorlands by disembarking his troops at Cramond.[3] By whatever route the central plain

---

[1] *Hist. Eccles.*, Bk. III, Chap. IV (ed. C. Plummer, Vol. I, p. 133).

[2] See Sir George Macdonald in *Journal of Roman Studies*, Vol. IX, pp. 133-5; also I. A. Richmond in *Kirkcudbright*, by J. Robison, pp. 16-7.

[3] For the evidence see Sir George Macdonald in *Proc. Soc. Ant. Scot.*, Vol. LII, pp. 252-3.

was reached, the advance thereafter, by the gap of Stirling, Perth, the valley of the Isla, and Strathmore, was straightforward and relatively unimpeded. It is marked to this day by the line of Roman entrenched posts through Strathmore, at Ardoch, Strageath, Inchtuthil and Raedykes, turning the Mounth at Normandykes in the valley of the lower Dee, and so on to Glenmailen in Auchterless, the most northerly identified camp of the legionaries.

The armies of the Cæsars never succeeded in establishing permanent control over "Caledonia stern and wild"; but where Rome failed with the sword she returned to conquer by the Cross. The earliest chapter in the Christianisation of what is now called Scotland will never be rightly understood until we grasp the fact that it was simply an epilogue to the long story of attempted Imperial domination. St. Ninian, the apostle of the Picts, was a Roman British provincial: his mission, like that of Ulfilas to the Goths very shortly before, was doubtless a detail in Imperial policy; and it followed the same line of penetration which the legions before had trod. From the monastic base which he established in 397 at *Candida Casa*, now Whithorn in Galloway, the mission led by St. Ninian advanced to the Clyde basin at Glasgow, thence traversed the central plain by St. Ninian's at Stirling, and so up Strathmore by Arbirlot and Dunnottar, turning the Mounth barrier, and penetrating into what is now Aberdeenshire and beyond.

Contrary to views long stubbornly maintained in the teeth of accumulating evidence, the work of St. Ninian was not left "in the air," nor did *Candida Casa* cease to function after its founder's death in 432. Ninian's labours were followed up along the same route in the fifth and sixth centuries by successors like St. Caranoc, St. Kentigern and St. Finbar—of whom the last penetrated into the remote north as far as Dornoch, while the others reached the uplands of Mar and the basin of the Deveron. Early in the eighth century we meet with a revival of the eastward access, by sea like the Emperor Severus five hundred years before, in the mission of St. Curitan (Boniface), who introduced the *cultus* of Blessed Peter into Pictland. Landing with his disciples at Invergowrie, St. Curitan established his monastic base at Restennet, and thence pushed forward along the well-worn route to end his days at Rosemarkie in Ross-shire, where the Iro-Pictish St. Moluag of Lismore (died 592) had laboured and found a grave before him.

It will have been seen that these successive Christian missions into Pictland followed well-defined strategic routes dictated by the fundamental and inevitable geographical conditions, and used by the Imperial legions centuries before. Upon this well-established line of religious and cultural penetration broke in, as a powerful diversion in flank, during the latter half of the sixth century, the Scotic mission headed by St. Columba. A moment's reflection will show how inconveniently Columba's headquarters, in the remote island of Iona, with Ireland as his unforgotten hinterland,[1] was placed for reaching and serving the Pictish tribes of eastern Scotland, separated from him by the great barrier of Drumalban. True, that barrier was not impassable: it was surmounted often enough, for example in Columba's time by St. Moluag, the Irish Pict, from his monastery at Lismore, and in the next century by St. Maelrubha, from Bangor of the Irish Picts and Abercrossan (Applecross);[2] while Columba himself more than once traversed the mountain ridge, both by the Great Glen and by the alternative route *via* the headwaters of the Tay. But for the Abbot of Iona the task was rendered greatly more difficult by the hostile relations that existed between Brude MacMaelchon, the Pictish High King at Inverness, and the intrusive Scotic Kingdom of Dalriada—now, after a recent smashing Pictish victory, clinging precariously and on sufferance to the mainland and islands of Argyll. Columba, as I understand him, was a politician first and an ecclesiastic afterwards: if my reading of the evidence be right, he identified himself, prominently and passionately, with the cause of his oppressed kinsfolk the Dalriads; and he did not, therefore, enjoy freedom of access into Pictland or the goodwill of its King. Long after Columba's death the dividing line of Drumalban continued, broadly speaking, to separate the Pictish and the Scotic Churches. It was not until the ninth century, with the Scotic ascendancy in Alba under the

---

[1] "The Irish are dearer to me than the rest of the men of the world," Columba is made to say in the *Lebar Brecc*.—See Anderson, *Early Sources of Scottish History*, Vol. I, p. 24.

[2] See the exhaustive paper on this Saint by Dr. Reeves in *Proc. Soc. Ant. Scot.*, Vol. III, pp. 258-96; also A. B. Scott in *Scottish Historical Review*, Vol. VI, pp. 260-80.

Alpin dynasty, that the Church founded by Columba, tying the Scotic flag to the Cross, extended its control throughout Pictland, and in its later hagiography vastly enlarged the reputation and the scope of its astute and masterful founder.

It is therefore apparent that throughout the early ecclesiastical history of Scotland the major dividing line has ever been Drumalban. The conclusion thus drawn from historical evidence is amply confirmed by the archæological material still available. In the present work[1] I have shown that the early Christian monuments of Scotland group themselves broadly into two quite distinct areas, and that the line of division between them is none other than Drumalban. But a good deal more underlies the archæological evidence than this. It will have been seen from what I have said above that Whithorn, and not Iona, is the real apostolic centre of Scotland. And not merely was Whithorn the headquarters from which successive bands of evangelists were launched into the remotest districts of Pictland: it was also, as is well known, a favourite starting point for missions to Ireland, and a school whither Irish monks thronged to receive their training.[2] So important a monastery must certainly have been a great cultural centre, from which art influences would radiate in ever widening ripples. That this was so in the case of Columba's monastery is well ascertained: we may trace the extension of the peculiar Christian art of Iona throughout the Hebrides, and can follow it also in its advance into Northumbria, where in the seventh and eighth centuries the Church of Iona inspired the brilliant Hiberno-Saxon illuminations of the Lindisfarne Gospels, and the distinctively Irish types of gravestone found at Hartlepool and Lindisfarne; and, blending at this point with other art influences, blossomed forth into such monumental triumphs as the Ruthwell and Bewcastle Crosses. Equally distinct, and not less far-flung, are the ramifications of the art influences emanating from Whithorn. Professor Baldwin Brown has remarked that the familiar Celtic wheeled cross is derived from the Chi-Rho monogram on inscribed monuments of the fifth and sixth

[1] See *infra*, pp. 73-8.
[2] See for the evidence of this, Skene, *Celtic Scotland*, Vol. II, pp. 46-9; also Scott, *Pictish Nation*, pp. 90-9.

centuries which still remain at Whithorn and the associated site of Kirkmadrine. "It is called Celtic," he observes of this form of cross-head, "because it is of very common use in the case of crosses in Ireland, but it is of course an importation from classical lands. Into the chronology of it, or the geographical route by which it reached the shores of Erin, no special inquiry seems to have been made. It is quite possible that the route was not a direct one, and that, like other elements in Irish Christianity, it was transmitted through Wales. . . . It is enough here to have indicated the early stages in the development of the Celtic cross-head, which need not be considered Irish in its origin. The Whithorn slab may be regarded as of special interest as a point of departure."[1] That *Candida Casa* was in fact the "point of departure" seems pretty obvious, in view of the known historical connections between St. Ninian's monastery and Ireland. The alternative suggestion of Wales is rendered improbable by the circumstance that, as Dr. Baldwin Brown himself points out, the Chi-Rho monogram is there extremely unusual; and when it occurs it is never in the Whithorn manner.

We have to think of Whithorn, then, as the great centre from which the type of cross now known as Celtic was introduced not only into Ireland (thence to be carried to Iona, and back from there to Northumbria), but also into Pictland, into Wales, and through Wales into Cornwall. Mr. W. G. Collingwood, in his recent most interesting book upon the Northumbrian crosses, boldly asserts that "all monumental art and craft in the north-west of Europe sprang from Northumbria"—including in that sweeping claim not merely the art of Iona (which gave its Christianity to Northumbria!) but also the art of Pictland in the east.[2] It would seem, however, that Mr. Collingwood has set the offspring in place of the parent. A view more in consonance with the historical and archæological evidence is that already set forth in essence by Professor Baldwin Brown as quoted above, namely, that Whithorn, the *Candida Casa* of St. Ninian, is the parent of the Celtic monumental cross alike in Pictland and in Ireland; and that this special cross form, as developed in Ireland, extended itself

[1]*Proc. Soc. Ant. Scot.*, Vol. LIII, pp. 221, 223.
[2]*Northumbrian Crosses of the Pre-Norman Age*, pp. 182-4.

through Iona to Northumbria, which in this respect at least was the receiver and not the giver. Picts, Irish and Northumbrians each modified the Celtic cross in their own way, and each superadded to the cross the special art-characteristics of their race. The Picts graved it on a slab, and surrounded it with their mysterious symbols and their sprightly and joyous animal forms. The Irish raised their cross free standing on a high shaft, and covered it with ornamental patterns and stately figure sculpture. The Northumbrians added their vine-scrolls and other elements showing classical influences explained by the known history of the early Anglian church.[1] But the position of *Candida Casa* as the starting point for all these monumental systems is unmistakably clear. The scene of St. Ninian's apostolic labours; mother-church of the Picts; nerve-centre of widespread missionary effort; the focus from which a great and beautiful monumental art extended itself over three countries: no more hallowed ground than Whithorn is to be found in all Scotland.

*   *   *   *   *   *   *   *

A word or two may be added about the character of St. Columba as portrayed in the following pages. That portrayal has roused strong resentment in certain quarters. Two of my critics in particular have made much ado by a massing together of phrases torn from their context:[2] such as "overbearing pride," "unscrupulous craft," "passionate vindictiveness," "intolerant and prejudiced," and so forth. I may be permitted to remark that it would have been only fair to exhibit the other side of the medal also. "Tender and lovable," "a great saint and churchman," "compassion for the weak," "warm-hearted sympathy with the sufferings of dumb animals," are epithets also to be found in my judgments about Columba's character. In any case no good purpose will be served by such an unrelated assemblage of passages

[1]This Anglian art in its turn reacted upon the art of Pictland, as is shown by the vine-scroll occurring on a Pictish sculptured cross-slab as far north as Hilton of Cadboll.

[2]Abbot Sir David Hunter Blair, O.S.B., in the course of an exceedingly able and courteous *critique* in *Scottish Historical Review*, Vol. XXIV, pp. 300-2; the Rev. C. L. Broun in *The Scottish Chronicle*, 9th September, 1927. Neither of these critics is always careful to reproduce my words with accuracy: indeed Abbot Hunter Blair in one case makes me use a word not to be found in the English language!

dealing with varied aspects and different periods in the development of
so highly complex a personality as I conceive Columba's to have been.
I would beg leave to refer such critics to what Gibbon has to say in
introducing his analysis of the character of the Emperor Constantine.
"By the impartial union of those defects which are confessed by his
warmest admirers and of those virtues which are acknowledged by his
most implacable enemies, we might hope to delineate a just portrait of
that extraordinary man, which the truth and candour of history should
adopt without a blush. But it would soon appear that the vain attempt
to blend such discordant colours, and to reconcile such inconsistent
qualities, must produce a figure monstrous rather than human, unless
it is viewed in its proper and distinct lights by a careful separation of
the different periods of the reign of Constantine."[1] Even so, I submit,
is the case of St. Columba. It must be apparent to all who study his
life—or indeed the life of any other personage who lived in the same
period—that the historical materials upon which a judgment must be
formed are often extremely doubtful and conflicting. But in the case
of Columba it does seem to me that the various early writers who have
described his personality, and the legends that have gathered round his
name, all combine to leave a singularly vivid and well-marked portrait
which it is impossible to ignore. What appear to be patent inconsist-
encies must be resolved as Gibbon invites us to resolve them in the
case of Constantine. It seems to me perfectly clear that as Columba
grew older he made a real conquest of himself. There can be no doubt
that in his earlier days he possessed a "natural character," in the words
of the Duke of Argyll, "which was full of strong and fierce emotions";[2]
and the gentler close portrayed in Adamnan's beautiful last chapter
suggests that in the evening of his days the passionate protagonist
came more and more to dwell in his inmost thoughts upon the burden
of his parting message to his flock—a message perhaps inspired by the
stormy memories of his own life: "These, O my children, are the last
words I address to you—that ye be at peace, and have unfeigned charity
among yourselves"!

[1] *Decline and Fall of the Roman Empire*, Chap. XVIII (ed. J. B. Bury, Vol. II, p. 202).

[2] See the passage quoted *infra*, p. 9.

ADDENDA TO THE SECOND EDITION.

P. 2, note 4 : *Knowledge of Greek in the Celtic Church.* A courteous French critic (M. J. Vendryes in *Revue Celtique,* Vol. XLIV, Nos. 1-2, p. 192) directs my attention to the very exhaustive paper on this subject by M. Esposito ("The Knowledge of Greek in Ireland during the Middle Ages") in *Studies,* Vol. I, pp. 665-83 ; *cf. Revue Celtique,* Vol. XXXIV, pp. 220-2 ; also *Phases of Irish History,* by Eoin MacNeill, pp. 243-4.

P. 7 : *The Battle of Cooldrevny.* Several of my critics have complained that I have said nothing about the story of the execution of Curnan (as told in the *"Annals of the Four Masters,"* ed. J. O'Donovan, Vol. I, pp. 190-3) as being a contributory cause to the dispute leading up to the battle. But I make it clear in the text that the Clan Niall "had discontents of their own against their suzerain." My purpose is with Columba, and my text had to be kept within manageable limits. Nor do I admit that the impression conveyed is a misleading one. It seems to me perfectly clear that Columba and his brooding over his wrongs were the dominating factor in the quarrel.

P. 12 : *Columba's austerities.* These are not in accordance with early Irish practice, and in the opinion of Dr. Reeves (*Adamnan,* 1874, p. 238) are probably an exaggeration of St. Columba's self-denial. Yet Adamnan in his second Preface writes :—*"Ieiunationum quoque et vigiliarum indefessis laboribus sine ulla intermissione die noctuque ita occupatus, ut supra humanum possibilitatem uniuscuiusque pondus specialis videretur operis"* (ed. Fowler, 1920, p. 87).

P. 13 : *The Picts.* As Mr. A. O. Anderson points out, reviewing Professor Watson's *History of the Celtic Place Names of Scotland* in *Aberdeen University Review,* Vol. XIV, p. 230, "the name *Picti* was territorial and not tribal." That the Picts occupied the land as far south as the wall of Hadrian seems to be the inference from Gildas, *De Excidio Britanniae,* sections 19 and 21 : *Scottorum Pictorumque greges . . . omnem aquilonalem extremamque terrae partem pro indigenis muro tenus capessunt"*; and *"Picti in extrema parte insulae tunc primum et deinceps requieverunt, praedas et contritiones nonnumquam facientes."* See the note of Mr. Hugh Williams *ad loc.,* in his edition (*Cymmrodorion Record Series,* No. 3), p. 48.

P. 14, note 2 : *Wroxeter.* The evidence discovered by earlier excavators that Viroconium had met a violent end has not been borne out by the more systematic uncovering of the ruins now proceeding. The town undoubtedly was burnt about the middle of the second century, but its end seems to have come about, early in the fifth century, by a peaceful withdrawal of the inhabitants, as at Silchester.   The coins found do not extend beyond the reign of Arcadius (395-408).   See J. P. Bushe-Fox's *Reports on the Excavations on the Site of the Roman Town at Wroxeter, 1912, p. 22; 1913, p. 2; 1914, p. 3;* and *cf. Journal of Roman Studies,* Vol. XIV, p. 227.

P. 15, note 5 : *Civilisation of the pagan Saxons.*   Even in regard to the Teutonic invaders the language used in this note probably conveys an under-estimate.   *Cf.* G. Baldwin Brown, *The Arts in Early England,* IInd ed., Vol. I, p. 33, speaking of "the weapons, implements, and objects of personal adornment found in Anglo-Saxon graves."   ("Some of these objects," he cautions, "especially those of glass, may be imported and not of native manufacture.")   "Though the taste and workmanship," so runs his verdict, "do not perhaps fully reach the standard of Scandinavia or Ireland, there are sword hilts and brooches in bronze and silver and gold with engraved enrichments and incrustations of coloured pastes and garnets, ornamented combs and cups of cunningly manipulated glass, wooden implements metal-mounted, and a store of miscellaneous objects, many of which afford profit-able material for study to the decorative artist of to-day."

P. 18, note 1 : *The pre-Columban Church in Dalriada.*   It is possible that, as Trenholme suggested (*Story of Iona,* p. 16), St. Ciaran of Clon-macnoise, who died apparently in 549, had also visited Dalriada.   Kilkerran in Kintyre seems to preserve his name; and as this was a very important Christian centre and royal burial place in pre-Columban days (see *infra,* p. 31, note 2), it is not at all improbable that it may have derived its distinction from a personal visit of the illustrious founder of Clonmacnoise.   Ciaran's dedications in Scotland almost seem to point to another example of the traditional line of penetration into Pictland, northward and eastward, of Ninian and his successors.   See Forbes, *Kalendars,* p. 436.

For Kilkerran see *Origines Parochiales Scotiae,* Vol. II, Part I, pp. 12-17.   The fine sculptured slabs are illustrated in James Drummond's *Sculptured Monuments of Iona and the West Highlands,* Plates LXXXI-III.

P. 19 : *Irish Picts.* Professor Watson, *Celtic Place Names of Scotland,* p 67, labours to explain away the Irish Picts, as also (pp. 174-9) the well documented Picts of Galloway.   Yet the early legends preserved in the *Pictish Chronicle* and in the Irish Nennius distinctly connect the race with Ireland. Adamnan, says Professor Watson (*op. cit.,* p. 74, note 2), "reserves *Picti* strictly for the *Cruithne* of Alba."   Yes, but in Book II, Chap. IX, he has a priest Iogenan, *gente Pictum,* living in Leinster.   *Cf.* also a significant passage in the Life of St. Cadroe (*Chronicles of the Picts and*

Scots, ed. W. F. Skene, p. 108) *"Igitur ad terram egressi, ut moris est, situm locorum, mores et habitum hominum explorare, gentem Pictaneorum reperiunt."*

P. 23, note 1 : *Aidan's coronation.* The Rev. C. L. Broun, writing in the *Scottish Chronicle,* 9th September, 1927, vigorously defends St. Columba's action in this matter. "As to 'interference in politics,' really Dr. Simpson writes like a twentieth century layman rebuking his parson for appearing on a political platform. Does he forget that St. Columba was on both sides descended from royal families in Ireland, and that he was one of the most prominent men of his nation, as well as the greatest Christian of his day in both Scotland and Ireland? Would he accuse Archbishop Stephen Langton of 'political interference' when he led the English nobility in demanding the signature of *Magna Carta*?" As a historical parallel this is about the most singularly misconceived that my critic could have chosen. Quite apart from the utter difference of the whole circumstances, Stephen Langton was entitled to deal in the *Magna Carta* crisis in his capacity as a feudal magnate, a status utterly unknown in Columba's time. Morover, to say nothing of his feudal status, the Primate of England, head of a see with such immense prestige and traditions inherited from the days of Augustine onward, had a long-conceded prescriptive right to counsel the King and to make his voice heard in high national concerns—a right which could never have been enjoyed by Columba, whose monastery at Iona was a foundation of not more than eleven years standing, and whose influence in Dalriadic affairs depended entirely on his own high birth and forceful personality. To apply the conceptions of the thirteenth century as a key to happenings in the sixth is surely no promising method of resolving a historical controversy.

P. 26 : *Adamnan's opinion of the Picts.* Mr. Gavin Tait in the course of a long and scholarly letter published in *Aberdeen Press and Journal,* 30th April, 1927, thus criticises my views on this question. "Dr. Simpson argues that St. Adamnan was an enemy of the Picts, because he calls them Gentiles and barbarians. The term Gentile denotes those who do not worship the God of Israel, and the term barbarian denotes those who are outside the pale of Graeco-Roman civilisation (*cf. Acts,* XXVIII, 2). In applying these epithets to the Picts of Columba's time (not of his own) Adamnan is simply calling them what they undoubtedly were." But were Adamnan or Columba, and were their countrymen the Scots of Dalriada, any more within "the pale of Graeco-Roman civilisation" than the Picts? Surely this argument destroys itself. Adamnan's "language about the Picts," continues Mr. Tait, "is very mild in comparison with that of St. Patrick and St. Gildas, who were both Britons. Patrick calls them 'the most vile and most worthless apostate Picts, a foreign nation who know not the Lord,' and Gildas says that they had 'more hair on their villainous faces than decent clothing on their bodies'; while the English biographer of St. Wilfred, at a time when the Picts were all Christians, does not scruple to call them 'the bestial nation of the Picts.' " Exactly: St. Patrick, St. Gildas, and Eddi all vigorously hated the Picts—a warrior race for whose military powers each and all had good reason to cherish a wholesome respect: and for the same reason Adamnan shared the prevailing prejudice, after the fashion of his gentler nature.

P. 27 : *Columba's alleged conversion of King Brude.* It is clear from such a passage as *Adamnan,* Bk. II, Chap. XXXIII, that, in spite of the alleged miraculous and certainly dramatic success of Columba's first interview with the Pictish monarch, the Druids were not dismissed from court but continued to exercise all their old influence over the King. Adamnan's evidence seems to me here decidedly to outweigh the later Bede, who had no access to Scotic records, and had not seen even Adamnan's *Life.* Another circumstance which shakes our confidence in Bede's account is that he asks us to believe that Columba's conversion of the Pictish King and people took place *before* his settlement on Iona (*Eccles. Hist.,* Bk. III, Chap. IV; Plummer's ed., Vol. I, p. 133) :—"*Venit autem Britanniam Columba regnante Pictis Brideo filio Meilochon, rege potentissimo, nono anno regni eius, gentemque illam verbo et exemplo ad fidem Christi convertit; unde et praefatam insulam ab eis in possessionem monasterii faciendi accepit.*" Something of a parallel to the relations between Brude and Columba seems to be found in those which existed between St. Ciaran of Clonmacnoise and King Diarmait MacCerball, who when Crown Prince gave him assistance in founding the monastery of Clonmacnoise, but afterwards continued to retain the Druids at his court.

P. 33 : *Culdees.* Another Culdee site, now otherwise forgotten, is suggested by a group of place-names near Methven. See Watson, *Celtic Place Names of Scotland,* pp. 266-7 : "near Methven in Perthshire are Drumbauchlie and Bachilton, also Culdeesland, all probably belonging to an old religious establishment."

P. 38 : *The Orkneys.* On the alleged Columban Church in the Orkneys the Rev. A. B. Scott has some shrewd criticism in *Scottish Historical Review,* Vol. II, p. 386. "Some historians have credited the Church of the northern isles to Columba. But the ministry of Columba or his disciples would neither have been acceptable nor popular in the islands. Archæologists and the *Historia Britonum* put it beyond doubt that the early islanders were Picts (see Dr. Anderson, *Orkneyinga Saga,* p. X). Columba and the Dalriad missionaries did not know the Pictish tongue.

Columba never went to the Orkneys, and so well aware was he of Orcadian hostilility to his missionaries that we find him appealing to Brude MacMaelchon to protect Cormac and others who had gone from Iona to the northern islands [see *Adamnan*, Bk. II, Chap. XLII]. Besides, Columba's Dalriad friends were the enemies of the Orcadian Picts. Aedhan MacGabhran wasted the Orkneys in 580, and apparently added them to the Dalriad Kingdom. Brude MacBile recovered the islands for the Picts, and drove out the Dalriad Scots in 682. If the Columban Church had any early influence in the Orkneys, it would only be during the short and insecure period of the Dalriad occupation. It is plain that the Columban Church does not account for that evidently popular, well-developed, and well-organised insular Church which is pointed to by Ari Fródi (*Islendingabók*) Dicuil (*De Mensura Orbis Terrarum*), and by the inscriptions, ornamentation, and symbols on the ancient stones. . . . Ninian's work explains the origin of the Church of the northern islands. Where are we to look for the base on which that church depended for its continuation? Ninian's *Candida Casa* is the only place, seeing that Iona is out of the question."

It should be noted that Joceline, *Vita Kentegerni*, Chap. XXXIV, states that St. Kentigern sent out missions to the Orkneys. This most valuable piece of evidence clearly points to the truth of Mr. Scott's contention that the Church of the northern archipelago was based upon *Candida Casa* and the Britons of Strathclyde, and not upon Iona and the Scots.

In addition to the Orcadian sites mentioned in the text, there are three chapels of St. Colm on the island of South Ronaldshay: one at Loch of Burwick, O.S. 6 in., Orkneys and Shetlands, Sheet CXXVI; one at Grimness (*ibid.*, Sheet CXXI) and one at Hoxa (*ibid.*, Sheet CXX). In Shetland, at Hillswick, Northmaven, "St. Colmis-kirk" is mentioned in 1574 (*Fasti Ecclesiae Scoticanae*, Vol. III, p. 439). Near it on the opposite side of the narrow isthmus is St. Magnus's Chapel and burial ground (O.S. *ut supra*, Sheet XXIV). Very often we find a Norse *dedication* thus planted close to an earlier Pictish *foundation*.

L. Dietrichson (*Monumenta Orcadica*, p. 10) states that he "believes he has seen beehive houses on the Brough of Birsay, around the ruins of the Norwegian church, no doubt the remains of a Celtic church dedicated to St. Columba." The Brough of Birsay accordingly has found its way into the list of alleged Columban sites collected by J. Mackinlay, *Ancient Church Dedications in Scotland (Non-Scriptural Dedications)* p. 48. But that these remains, even if they are those of a Celtic church, should be associated with Columba, appears to be quite an arbitrary conclusion on Dietrichson's part. The later (twelfth century) church on the Brough is said to have been under the invocation of St. Peter—*History of the Orkney Islands*, by Rev. Geo. Barry, 1805, p. 33.

P. 39 : *Dedication to the Apostle Peter.* The obliteration of St. Drostan by St. Peter took place at other places besides Deer. For example, close to St. Drostan's church-site at Rothiemay is St. Peter's well.

Similar cases of the obliteration of the real founder of a church by a dedication to St. Peter are noted by Baldwin Brown, *The Arts in Early England,* Vol. I (IInd ed.), pp. 277-8. "When the late Bishop Lightfoot undertook his northern diocese he found to his surprise that there was not a single church within the bounds of Durham county dedicated to Aidan of Lindisfarne (*Leaders in the Northern Church,* p. 49). Aidan himself had built a little oratory on Holy Island, which his successor renewed. This would almost certainly have been known by Aidan's honoured name, but we learn that after the departure of the Scottish missionaries Archbishop Theodore consecrated it under the Roman invocation of St. Peter. Most of the other Aidan churches, that must have been numerous enough in the north, were doubtless after the Synod of Whitby treated in a similar manner."

P. 41, note 2 : *Bede's judgement about Columba.* In marked contrast to this language, Bede emphatically describes Adamnan as *vir bonus et sapiens, et scientia scripturarum nobilissime instructus . . . vir unitatis ac pacis studiosissimus* (*Eccles. Hist.,* Bk. V, Chap. XV—Plummer's ed., Vol. I, pp. 315-6). Such a verdict stands in complete agreement with all that we know otherwise about Adamnan's character, and indeed with the evidence self-revealed in his own writings. Bede, it is thus clear, was careful and measured in his judgments; and his curious language about Columba was not chosen without a meaning.

P. 45 : *A Church near Coleraine.* In the Preface to the *Altus Prosator* it is called *Ross Torathair,* a name otherwise unknown. Mr. Sam Henry, Sandelford, Coleraine, has been good enough to write me that the traditions of the neighbourhood identify this church with the ancient church always called Camus or Cambos, from the bend in the river Bann. It is the *monasterium Cambas* of *Adamnan,* Bk. I, Chap. XXXV : see Reeves, ed. 1874, p. 266. Mr. Henry very kindly sends me photographs of a sculptured cross-shaft, probably of the tenth century, and a medieval baptismal font, both of which still remain in the churchyard.

P. 52 : *St. Aidan.* M. J. Vendryes, discussing my book in *Revue Celtique,* Vol. XLIV, Nos. 1-2, p. 190, reminds me that before the mission of Aidan, King Edwin of Northumbria had already been converted through the agency of his wife, the Kentish Princess Ethelburga, and her chaplain Paulinus, who was consecrated to the See of York in 625. M. Vendryes rightly observes how greatly the spread of Christianity in those early times was furthered by women : he instances Clotilda, the wife of Clovis King of the Franks, and Theodelinda, the wife of Agilulf, King of the Lombards.

P. 58: *St. Niniah's Bishopric.* Mr. Anderson has since developed this idea very considerably in an important article in *Aberdeen University Review,* Vol. XIV, pp. 227-34. The difficulty seems to be that the rule was for the diocese to shape itself in accordance with the provincial boundary, whereas, according to Mr. Anderson's theory, the reverse would have happened in Strathclyde.

There is a good discussion of the growth of the diocesan organisation in the West in Baldwin Brown, *Arts in Early England,* Vol. I, (IInd. ed.), pp. 136-9: see also p. 155.

P. 58: *Scoto-Pictish relationships.* The story told in *Adamnan,* Bk. II, Chap. XXIII, of how a Pictish nobleman, exiled on the Scotic island of Islay, was murdered by his host, seems also to provide a commentary on the relations between the two peoples. *Cf.* also the predatory expedition of the Picts against Islay in 565, told in the old life of St. Comgall (*Vitae Sanctorum Hiberniae,* ed. Plummer, Vol. II, p. 11).

P. 61: *The Ruthwell and Bewcastle Crosses.* In no less emphatic and satisfactory a manner than the Bewcastle and Ruthwell Crosses, a critical analysis of the Lindisfarne Gospels will be found to illumine the composite sources of early Northumbrian Christian culture. The date and origin of this famous codex are set forth in the colophon at the end of St. John's Gospel. Added in the tenth century by a priest called Aldred, this colophon states that the codex was written by Eadfrith, Bishop of Lindisfarne, 698-721. A detailed and most masterly examination of the art-characteristics and relationships of the sumptuously illuminated manuscript has been made by Professor Baldwin Brown, *The Arts in Early England,* Vol. V, pp. 329-96. While the general style of the work is distinctly Irish, classical or rather Hellenistic models—just as in the figure sculpture on the two crosses—have inspired the finely executed portraits of the four evangelists, so different from the crude human figures found even in the best Irish manuscripts. Classical influences appear also in the architectural framing of the Eusebian canons, and more generally in a strong feeling for balanced grouping in the decorative schemes. Again, the Anglian spirit, as on the two crosses, is shown by the delight in sportive bird and beast forms, and the surpassing skill with which these are rendered. The bird represented, it is specially interesting to note, is the cormorant still so common on the rocky shores of Lindisfarne. Generally speaking, the Lindisfarne Codex contrasts with the riotous exuberance and unrestrained fantasy of its two great Irish counterparts, the Book of Durrow and the Book of Kells, by a certain sense of austerity and restraint, in which both classical influences and the Anglian *ethos* have combined.

P. 64: *Elachnave*. Professor Watson, *op. cit.*, argues at much length that Hinba should be identified with Jura. But a serious objection to this view seems to lie in the fact that no church bearing Columba's name is found on this island. Professor Watson says that Hinba "appears to have lain in the track of vessels coming from Ireland, at least that seems to be the inference from the fact that Comgall, Cainnech, Brendan and Cormac, coming from Ireland to visit Columba, found him in Hinba." But surely this is forced reasoning. They would seek out Columba in whatever place he happened at the time to be.

P. 65: *Columban sites in Lewis*. Between Lewis and Skye lie the basaltic Shiant Isles, on one of which is said to have been "a chapel dedicated to St. Columba"—J. Macculloch, *Description of the Western Islands of Scotland*, Vol. I (1819), p. 435. Macculloch calls the island with the chapel *Eilan-a-kily*; but from his description it is evident that the island he refers to is the one now called *Eilean-an-Tighe*, at the north end of which a nameless graveyard is marked on the O.S. Map (6 in., Lewis, Sheet 49).

P. 66: *Canna*. The parsonage of Canna belonged to the Abbot of Iona, and the vicarage to the Bishop of the Isles. See *Origines Parochiales*, Vol. II, Part I, p. 339. For the curious structure called "The Altar," and the west end of the island, see *Proc. Soc. Ant. Scot.*, Vol. XXXIII, pp. 133-40.

P. 67: *Columban sites in Islay*. In *Proc. Soc. Ant. Scot.*, Vol. XVI, p. 266, it is stated that "there are (or were) three churches dedicated to St. Columba in Islay." The third is identified by J. M. Mackinlay, *Ancient Church Dedications in Scotland (Non-Scriptural)*, p. 54, with the chapel site at Laggan (see Graham, *Carved Stones of Islay*, p. 42); but no authority is stated. No designation is given to the chapel in the O.S. Map (6 in., Argyllshire, Sheet CCXIX).

P. 68: *Columban sites in Kintyre*. A grant made by Dufgal, son of Syfyn, to the monks of Paisley, dated at Paisley Abbey on Palm Sunday, 1261, conveys to them the "*capella Sancti Columbe que sita est juxta castrum meum de Schepehinche*"—*Registrum Monasterii de Passelet*, p. 121. Until recently it has been usual to assume that the chapel thus referred to is the fine thirteenth century church which still stands as a well preserved ruin on the sea shore below Skipness Castle. But this church has always been known as *Kilbrannan*, St. Brendan's Church. It was sought to meet this difficulty either by supposing "a very unclerkly slip of the pen" on the part of the scribe who drew out the charter of 1261: or alternatively that the chapel had been under a double invocation (see Capt. T. P. White, *Archæological Sketches in Scotland, Kintyre*, pp. 180-2). Recently however the mystery has been brilliantly solved by Messrs. Angus Graham and

R. G. Collingwood, who, in the course of a most interesting paper on Skip-ness Castle (*Proc. Soc. Ant. Scot.,* Vol. LVII, pp. 266-87), have shown that part of the wall of a small thirteenth century detached chapel is embodied in the later *enceinte* of the castle. This fragment undoubtedly represents "the chapel of St. Columba beside the Castle of Schepehinche" as described in the charter of 1261. That being so, we have here a highly significant juxtaposition of ecclesiastical sites. The early ecclesiastical centre was a cell of St. Brendan of Clonfert (*cf. infra.,* p. 18, note 1), now represented by the thirteenth century church which bears his name; but when the lord of the manor built for himself a private chapel in the precinct of his castle, he placed it under the patronage of the then popular St. Columba. Here, therefore, we have a very clear example of a medieval *dedication* to Columba, under manorial influence, taking its place along side the original Celtic *foundation* of St. Brendan.

P. 68-69 : *Church sites of St. Colm of Buchan and Caithness.* The O.S. Map. (6 in., Aberdeenshire, Sheet XC) marks the "site of St. Columba's chapel" within an enclosure south of Abergeldie Castle. But in 1736 this was St. Valentine's chapel—see *Ant. Abdn. and Banff,* Vol. II, p. 85. If the attribution to St. Columba be older, then we have probably another disguised foundation of St. Colm—who certainly penetrated as far west as Birse. This is the view adopted by the Rev. John Stirton, *Crathie and Braemar,* pp. 14, 16.

P. 71 : *Inchcolm.* For the Celtic oratory see also J. Wilson Paterson in *Proc. Soc. Ant. Scot.,* Vol. LX, pp. 229-30.

P. 71 : *Columban Church sites in Bernicia.* An interesting case at Colmslee, Melrose, is discussed by Mackinlay, *op. cit.,* p. 47, who points out that this is probably a dedication resulting from St. Aidan's mission to the Northumbrians : the church at all events belonged to the monastery founded by him at Old Melrose.

P. 73, note 3 : *Anwoth.* Remember that this place is within the territory of the ancient Picts of Galloway.

P. 82 : *St. Columba's Pillow.* So a cross was afterwards carved on the stone at Clonmacnoise which St. Ciaran used as a seat : *usque hodie colitur, posita ibi cruce Christi*—Plummer, *Vitae Sanctorum Hiberniae,* Vol. I, p. 201.

P. 83 : *Evidence linking Ninianic sites with the Celtic Church.* Another important case is St. Ninian's chapel at Navidale. Professor Watson him-self points out (*op. cit.,* p. 250) that the place-name Navidale contains the early Celtic church term *nemed* (*nemeton*), *sanctuary,* and is aware that in the seventeenth century Sir Robert Gordon (*Genealogical History of the Earl-*

dom of Sutherland, pp. 3, 135), states that here "in old tymes ther wes a sanctuarie" or "place of refuge," i.e., "a place that had the right of sanctuary or girth.   The formation," says Dr. Watson, "is Norse, the second part being Norse *dalr,* a dale.   The Norsemen found the *nemed* there as an important place, and named the dale after it."   Here then, on Dr. Watson's own showing, is an early Celtic religious site of proved importance at the time of the Viking penetration : and it is associated with the name of St. Ninian.   Could the evidence be clearer?

For Navidale see *New Statistical Account,* Vol. XV (Sutherland), p. 201. Near the churchyard is St. Ninian's Well, *Tober'inian* (Scott, *Pictish Nation,* p. 85).   The site is on a peninsulated rock strikingly similar to that of St. Ninian's chapel at Dunnottar Castle.

P. 86 : *The Skeabost Stone.*   In the first edition I followed *Proc. Soc. Ant. Scot.,* as cited, in stating that the stone was 2 miles from Skeabost Bridge.   I owe the correction to the kindness of the Rev. A. Campbell-Fraser, Bedlington Vicarage, Northumberland.   The stone is rightly marked on the revised (1907) edition of the O.S. Map (1 inch, Inverness-shire, Sheet 80).   Mr. James S. Richardson, Inspector of Ancient Monuments for Scotland, sends me a drawing which shows that the full length of this stone above ground is 4 feet 5 inches, and that on the lower portion, not shown in Fig. 18, the mirror and the comb symbols are visible.

Mr. Richardson has also kindly sent me drawings of three other symbol stones, not yet published, from the Isles.   One from Fiskavaig, Skye, now in the National Museum of Antiquities, Edinburgh, has the double disc and Z-rod with the crescent and V-rod below.   The second, at Dunvegan Castle, Skye, has the crescent and V-rod above a double concentric circle.   The third stone, on the island of Raasay, has an equal armed and shafted cross within a square frame of peculiar design, rather suggestive of *Candida Casa* influence, and below it the "tuning fork" and crescent and V-rod symbols.   All these stones will be described by the Royal Commission on Ancient Monuments in their forthcoming Report on the Outer Hebrides, Skye, and the Smaller Isles.

P. 91 : *The Bachuill Mor.*   Such a pastoral staff is accurately described by Joceline, who, in his *Vita Kentegerni,* Chap. XIII, speaks of that Saint's *bachuill* in the following words : *"et virgam pastoralem non spericam etiam auratam ac gemmatam, sicut nunc temporis est cernere, sed de simplici ligno, tantum reflexam."*   The twelfth century hagiographer must have found this accurate description of a Celtic pastoral staff, so unlike the medieval crosier, in the *"codiculum alium, stilo Scottico dictatum,"* which he tells us in his Prologue that he used.

P. 97 : *The Kilmorie Stone.*   Mr. W. G. Collingwood, in his recent work, *Northumbrian Crosses of the Pre-Norman Age,* pp. 92-102 and 103, has discussed this stone.   He claims that Anglian traditions are revealed in the hammer-headed cross form, also in the patterns of the scroll work and plaits.   The district, of course, was one peculiarly subject to Anglian influence in the later pre-Conquest period (*cf. infra.,* p. 72).   "Until the Edwardian wars," pertinently observes Mr. Collingwood (p. 98), "the Solway united rather than severed its two shores."   He appears to regard the carving on both sides of the stone as contemporary, and would date it "early in the eleventh century."

P. 97 : *St. Martin's Cross.*   On 9th August, 1927, I was privileged in being present at the discovery and decipherment, by Professor R. A. S. Macalister, of an inscription in Irish letters carved at the base of the shaft on the western face.   Professor Macalister's provisional reading and translation is as follows :—

OROIT DO

GILLACRIST

DORINGNE

T CHROS

SA

"A prayer for Gilla-crist, who made this cross."

On the same occasion there was consummated the process of putting together, under Professor Macalister's expert guidance, the fragments of St. John's Cross, the most beautiful of all the crosses remaining at Iona. The cross, as now restored to its complete form, closely resembles the Kildalton Cross (Fig. 64), but is even finer in its proportions and delicacy of enrichment.   See for these recent discoveries at Iona Professor Macalister's letters in the *Glasgow Herald,* 12th August and 22nd September, 1927.

The Historical Saint Columba.

S T. COLUMBA, the apostle of the Scots in Alba, but not of the country now called Scotland, was born on Thursday, 7th December, 521,[1] in the little village of Gartan,[2] on the shores of the loch of the same name, amid the wild mountains of Donegal. He belonged to the race of Conall Gulban,[3] and on both sides could boast royal descent. His father, Phelim MacFergus, was great-grandson of the famous Irish *Ardrigh* or High King, Niall of the Nine Hostages, who reigned from 379 to 405. Niall, it is interesting to remember, sat on the throne of Tara at the time when the young lad Patrick, afterwards to become the apostle of Ireland, was carried captive into Antrim from Britain by a crew of pirates. Columba's mother, Eithne, was descended from the royal house of Leinster. We have always to bear in mind the fact that Columba was of regal blood both on the spear and on the spindle side, for in ancient Celtic society this advantage increased enormously his political and spiritual prestige. The Old Irish Life of Columba remarks that had he not chosen to become a soldier of Christ he might have been High King of Erin.[4]

The child was baptised[5] by the name of Colum, Latinised as

[1] For the date see A. O. Anderson, *Early Sources of Scottish History*, vol. I., p. 31, note 4. On that same day died St. Buite, founder of Monasterboice.

[2] For Irish localities connected with Columba see Map, Fig. 1. The ecclesiastical remains at Gartan are described by Bishop W. Reeves in his edition of Adamnan's *Life of St. Columba* ("Historians of Scotland" ed., with notes by W. F. Skene, and a translation by Bishop A. P. Forbes, 1874, pp. 224-5). This is the edition of Dr. Reeves' great work which I have generally used, but I have also consulted where necessary the original edition (1857). In these notes the two editions are cited by their respective dates, thus : Reeves, *Adamnan*, 1857, or 1874. In reference to Adamnan's text I have followed the divisions into chapters given in Dr. J. T. Fowler's edition (1920).

[3] From which the district of Tyrconnel takes its name.

[4] *The Old Irish Life of St. Columba*, transl. W. M. Hennessy in Skene's *Celtic Scotland*, vol. II., p. 474. See also § 1 of O'Donnell's *Life of Columcille*, ed. A. O'Kelleher and G. Schoepperle, p. 3.

[5] At *Tulach Dubhglaise*, now Temple Douglas, between Gartan and Letterkenny. See Reeves, *Adamnan*, 1874, pp. xxxiii.-iv., lvi.

Columba, the dove: after generations knew him as *Colum-kille*, "Columba of the cell or church," because—so an old Irish source beautifully explains—"he so frequently came forth from the cell where he read the Psalms in order to greet the neighbouring children, who would say among themselves, 'has our little dove come to-day from his cell?'" We are also told that he had a nickname among his contemporaries, namely, *Crimthann,* the wolf or fox—a designation which well accords with the combination of ferocity and craft that formed a marked feature in his highly complex and many-tinted character.[1] The old priest, Cruithnechan MacCellechain,[2] who baptised him, in accordance with Celtic custom became his foster-father; and with him at Kilmacrenan, on the River Lennan, the boy remained until he was old enough to be sent as a pupil to the great St. Finnian or Finbar at his school of Moville, near the head of Strangford Lough in County Down. St. Finbar himself, it is important to remember, had been trained at *Candida Casa,* the first Christian settlement in what is now Scotland, founded by St. Ninian, the apostle of the northern Britons and the Picts, at Whithorn in Galloway in the year 397,[3] while southern Britain was still a Roman province. At Moville the young Columba remained until he reached the status of a deacon. Thereafter he went to Leinster, where he studied literature and music under an aged bard called Gemman.[4] His next move was to the famous monastic school of

---

[1] Mr. A. O. Anderson has suggested to me that " Colum, not Crimthan, was the nickname, assumed as a monastic name: indeed, I believe that the original nickname was Columcille in full, 'church pigeon.' "

[2] *"Spectabilis vitae vir"*—*Adamnan,* Bk. III., Chap. II. The name Cruithnechan suggests Pictish descent.

[3] The year in which *Candida Casa* was founded—the first authentic date in the history of Christianity in Scotland—is established by a passage in Ailred's *Life of St. Ninian*—a work written up in the twelfth century from older sources—in which it is stated that when Ninian was engaged in building his church he heard of the death of his master, St. Martin of Tours, the founder of Celtic missionary monasticism—*Lives of St. Ninian and St. Kentigern,* ed. Bishop A. P. Forbes, p. 144.

[4] According to the *Amra Choluimbchille* (ed. W. Stokes in *Revue Celtique*, Vol. XX., p. 405), " he learned Greek grammar: he used to converse with the grammarians of the Greeks." For a discussion upon the study of Greek in the Celtic Church see G. T. Stokes, *Proceedings of the Royal Irish Academy*, Third Series, Vol. II. (1891-3), pp. 177-202. Some knowledge of Greek is clearly evident in the language of Adamnan's writings.

Clonard,[1] on the Boyne, where he was ordained a priest.[2] He then transferred himself to the monastery presided over by St. Mobhi at Glasnevin, on the River Finglass near Dublin: but his sojourn here was cut drastically short by the great pestilence of 543, the same "yellow plague" which had scourged the Eastern Empire under Justinian in the preceding year, and is so vividly described by the Byzantine historian Procopius.[3] Its ravages depleted the monastery at Glasnevin to such an extent that St. Mobhi closed his establishment down. Columba now migrated to his ancestral home in Ulster. Here at Derry, the "place of the oaks," within thirty miles of his birthplace, in 546,[4] he planted his first monastery, on ground made over to him by his own tribe, the Clan Niall. With that tenacious love of place which is so characteristic of the Celt, Columba always held Derry in peculiar regard,

[1]Dr. J. T. Fowler, in his edition of Adamnan (ed. 1920, p. 46) gives an interesting description of Clonard, which he calls " the most famous of all the great schools of the sixth century."

As Dr. Skene has shown (*Celtic Scotland*, vol. II., pp. 45-52), the rapid development of monasticism throughout Ireland in the sixth century was fostered from two British centres: St. Ninian's foundation of *Candida Casa*, and the contemporary church of Wales (associated with the names of St. David, St. Gildas, and St. Cadoc) the descendant of the Christian community in the Romano-British province. It is very interesting to note that while one of Columba's instructors, St. Finbar of Moville, had been trained at *Candida Casa*, the other, St. Finnian of Clonard—an Irish Pict—had been a student at Kilmuine, or Menevia (now St. David's) under the three Welsh saints above-mentioned. Thus Columba united in himself both the great missionary currents from Britain that had so deeply influenced Irish Christianity.

[2]Columba never became a bishop, remaining a presbyter-abbot all his days. In the Celtic Church a bishop enjoyed nothing corresponding to what we know as diocesan authority. His duties were confined to ordination; and if attached to a monastery he was subject to its abbot, even if the latter were only a simple priest, as Columba was. Yet the episcopal office was held in high veneration, and even a man so conscious of his own authority as Columba delighted to show honour to a bishop. See *Adamnan*, Book I., chap. xliv., from which it appears that the right to celebrate mass alone, without a concelebrant, was accorded to the episcopal status.

For the curious story of Columba's disappointment at not being ordained a bishop *per saltum*, see the *Martyrology of Oengus*, ed. W. Stokes, p. 73. (In citing this work I have used Stokes' second edition, published by the Henry Bradshaw Society in 1905.)

[3]See Gibbon, *Decline and Fall of the Roman Empire*, end of chap. xliii (ed. J. B. Bury, vol. IV., pp. 436-40). The *Annals of the Four Masters* (ed. J. O'Donovan, vol. I., p. 183) refer to it under this year as "an extraordinary universal plague throughout the world, which swept away the noblest third part of the human race." In O'Donnell's Irish *Life*, ed. O'Kelleher and Schoepperle, § 75 (p. 63), the malady is described as "the jaundice of the colour of stubble."

[4]The date is given in *Annals of Ulster*, ed. W. M. Hennessy, Vol. I., p. 51, corrected by Anderson, *Early Sources*, Vol. I., p. 10. Nothing now remains of Columba's monastery except an ancient well called after his name.

and his thoughts often wistfully turned to it amid the bitterness of exile in Iona. On such occasions his passionate longing for the monastery of his first creation would find vent in a lyrical outburst[1] : —

> " Were the tribute of all Alba mine,
> From its centre to its border,
> I would prefer the site of one house
> In the middle of fair Derry.
> The reason I love Derry is
> For its quietness, for its purity,
> And for its crowds of white angels
> From the one end to the other.
> The reason why I love Derry is
> For its quietness, for its purity,
> Crowded full of heaven's angels
> Is every leaf of the oaks of Derry.
> My Derry, my little oak-grove,[2]
> My dwelling, and my little cell.
> Oh, eternal God in heaven above !
> Woe be to him who violates it."

Between the foundation of Derry in 546[3] and his exile to Iona in 563, Columba planted several other monasteries, notably Durrow[4] in central Ireland, on the borders of King's County and West Meath, and

---

[1] Reeves, *Adamnan*, 1857, p. 288. The poem, which is attributed to Columba, is a metrical record of his Irish foundations. Its language shows that it is of great antiquity, "although there is internal evidence to prove that it was composed in an after age." But there is abundant material to prove Columba's special affection for Derry, and the extract here quoted beautifully expresses his feelings.

[2] In O'Donnell's *Life*, ed. O'Kelleher and Schoepperle, § 89 (pp. 83-5), is a pleasing story of Columba's fondness for the oak-groves of Derry. He deflected the orientation of a church he was building in order to avoid the necessity of cutting down some of the trees. "And this is the quatrain he made after going into exile in Alba, and it proveth that naught was so grievous to him as to cut the grove of Derry:—

> ' Though I am affrighted, truly,
> By death and by Hell ;
> I am more affrighted, frankly,
> By the sound of an axe in Derry in the west.' "

[3] While presiding over his school at Derry, Columba is said to have paid a visit to Tours, where rested the body of St. Martin, the pioneer of Celtic missionary monasticism. But the chronology of the legend is impossible. See Reeves, *Adamnan*, 1874, p. 233. Later fabulists added a journey to Rome.

[4] Apart from grave-slabs, the remains at Durrow are now reduced to St. Columkille's Well and St. Columkille's Cross, a noble High Cross, dating probably from the early tenth century. See A. C. Champneys, *Irish Ecclesiastical Architecture*, pp. 85-6, and Plate **XXXIX**.

Kells[1] in the north-west corner of Meath. It should be noted in passing that neither of the two famous illuminated manuscripts associated with these religious houses—the Book of Durrow and the Book of Kells—is as old as Columba's time, although in each case tradition claims him as the author.[2] Columba certainly was a great transcriber. Later authorities asserted that he wrote with his own hand no less than 300 copies of the Gospels, and left one copy to each of the churches which he founded.[3]

In 561 occurred the central crisis in Columba's life, the event that determined his whole future career. By this time he was forty years of age, in the full powers of a vigorous body and splendid presence, with an active, dominating intellect, masterful and overbearing in temper, vindictive often and violently irascible, yet strangely tender and lovable withal—a character, in a word, as mighty, as arresting, and as changeable in its moods as the sea that embosoms the island of his exile. Already, moreover, he was famed throughout Ireland as a great saint and churchman, a golden-mouthed preacher of Christ, a mighty organiser of monasteries, *multarum columna ecclesiarum*.[4] But Columba could never forget that he was also a prince of the blood-royal of Ireland—"a king's son of reddened valour," as St. Cormac is said to have styled him on one occasion.[5] He was keenly interested and closely implicated in all the political movements of his time, and amid

[1] Kells, which in the ninth century (when Iona was suffering from the Viking ravages) became the metropolitan monastery of the Columban Church in Ireland, possesses a group of very important ecclesiastical remains, all dating from subsequent to this period. They include a well preserved round tower, mentioned as early as 1076 (" the steeple of Cennanus " —*Annals of Ulster*, ed. W. M. Hennessy, vol. II., p. 29); a building known as St. Columkille's House, which forms a complete miniature monastic establishment under one roof, with chapel, refectory, and dormitory each on one storey; a High Cross in the churchyard inscribed *Crux Patricii et Columbe*; another High Cross in the market place; the shaft of a broken cross in the churchyard; and an unfinished cross, also in the churchyard. See Champneys, *Irish Ecclesiastical Architecture*, pp. xxxii., 36, 40-2, 52, 57, 59, 78, 83, 86, 88, 89, 90, 92, 94, 121, 194-5, 208, 225, 230, and Plates XIX., XXVI., XLI.

[2] They are not earlier than the end of the seventh century. See Sir E. Maunde Thompson, *Introduction to Greek and Latin Palæography*, ed. 1912, p. 374: *cf.* Champneys, *op. cit.*, p. 213.

[3] In Adamnan's time the monastery of Iona still possessed *libris stylo ipsius descriptis*, which were believed to have miraculous powers.—*Adamnan*, Bk. II., Chap. XLIV.

[4] *Adamnan*, Bk. III., Chap. XXIII. (Fowler's ed., p. 184.)

[5] See Reeves, *Adamnan*, 1857, p. 269.

these constant excitements the turbulent blood of generations of hard-fighting ancestors, with all the bitter unreasoning factiousness of the Celt, would surge uncontrollably through his pulsing veins. More-over, in his strangely mingled character Columba united a reputation for sanctity with that quality of unscrupulous craft that earned him the nickname, *Crimthann,* "fox." While staying with his master, Finbar of Moville, he had surreptitiously gained access to a codex of the Gospels that he wanted to transcribe. Manuscripts were valuable in those early days,[1] and so the matter was carried before the High King, Diarmait MacCerball[2] (544-65), who only recently had granted Columba the ground for his monastery at Kells. King Diarmait decided against Columba, and ordered him to hand over to Finbar the copy of the book that he had made. "To every cow belongs her calf"— so ran his famous judgment— "and to every book its son-book." This is probably the first law of copyright recorded in history.[3]

The sentence thus recorded against him awoke all the passionate vindictiveness latent in Columba's soul. Blinded to every other consideration by the mad lust for revenge, he set himself to organise a rebellion of his kinsmen, the Clan Niall, against their sovereign King Diarmait. In appealing to the warlike passions of the turbulent Ulster-men, he could use all his own unrivalled and compelling eloquence, all

---

[1] "The privilege of obtaining copies of sacred writings in ancient times was eagerly sought for, and sometimes grudgingly given or absolutely refused."—H. C. Lawlor, *The Monastery of St. Mochaoi of Nendrum,* p. 51.

[2] Diarmait, son of Fergus Cerball, was a distant relative of Columba. See the genealogical table in Reeves, *Adamnan,* 1874, p. xliv.

[3] The famous *Cathach,* or " Battler " of Columba—which, with the magnificent silver shrine made for it at the end of the eleventh century, is now preserved in the Museum of the Royal Irish Academy, is reputed traditionally to have been the identical transcript about which the quarrel arose. It is a copy of the Psalter not the Gospels, and is written in a plain, almost unadorned, half-uncial hand. This fact, together with the extraordinary veneration in which the codex was held so far back as the eleventh century—despite its small intrinsic merits—have led to the belief that the manuscript may perhaps really be a genuine product of Columba's pen. See Professor H. J. Lawlor's paper in *Proc. Royal Irish Academy,* vol. XXXIII., Section C., No. 11 (1916), pp. 241-436. A page of the *Cathach* is illustrated at Fig. 3. The whole story of Finbar's codex, the quarrel with Columba, King Diarmait's judgment, the battle of Cooldrevny, and Columba's exile to Iona, has been exhaustively and critically analysed by Professor Lawlor in his paper, above mentioned, on the *Cathach.* Dr. Lawlor establishes beyond question the substantial authenticity of the story.

his Irishman's joy over a good rousing grievance, as well as the enormous personal influence which his dynastic position gave him. And Columba did not appeal in vain. Maddened by what they regarded as an insult to their kinsman, and a member of their ruling house, the Clan Niall, who had discontents of their own against their suzerain, rushed impetuously to arms; and at Cooldrevny, between Drumcliff and Sligo,[1] they won a bloody victory over the High King Diarmait. But "the wrath of man worketh not the righteousness of God"; and in thus instigating civil war Columba had overshot the mark. Blood had been shed, and he, a man of God, was the guilty cause. In the eyes of his fellow clerics his position was seriously shaken; and by working on their outraged feelings King Diarmait was able to gain his revenge for the defeat of Cooldrevny. At his instigation a national convention of the Irish clergy assembled in the patrimonial territory of the King at Teltown in Meath,[2] and Columba was ex-communicated. On the intercession of St. Brendan of Birr the sentence was afterwards withdrawn: but Columba, feeling that public opinion was against him, accepted the advice of his "soul-friend" or confessor, St. Molaise of Devenish in Lough Erne, who told him to make himself scarce, and hinted that he might ease his burdened conscience by winning in foreign lands as many souls for Christ as the lives thrown away in the frivolous quarrel that culminated in the slaughter of Cooldrevny. So it came to pass that, two years after the battle, Columba shook the dust of Ireland from his unwilling feet, and taking with him on the apostolic pattern twelve disciples, passed over to join his kinsmen, the Scots who had colonised Argyll.[3] As often, his sorrow found utterance in song :—

[1] For the locality of this place see Fowler, *Adamnan*, p. 247 (Dr. C. Plummer's note).

[2] An ancient seat of royalty between Kells and Navan. The remains of the great circular rath, about one hundred paces in diameter, may still be seen. The Irish monarch was sometimes styled *Righ Tailtenn*, King of Teltown. See Reeves, *Adamnan*, 1874, pp. 285-6, and Fowler, *Adamnan*, pp. 225-6.

[3] Adamnan, in his preface, glosses over the exile of his patron very tactfully:—"*Hic anno secundo post Culedrebinae bellum, aetatis vero suae xlii., de Scotia* [i.e., Ireland] *ad Britanniam pro Christo peregrinari volens emigravit.*" In the body of his work, however (Book III., chap. iii.), he vouchsafes a few guarded particulars: "*cum a quodam synodo pro quibusdam veniabilibus et tam excusabilibus causis, non recte ut post in fine claruit, sanctus excommunicaretur Columba,*" etc.

" I am filled with wealth, without Erin,
    Did I think it sufficient,
In the unknown land of my sojourn,
    Of sadness and distress.
Alas, the voyage that was enjoined me,
    O King of Secrets,
For having gone myself
    To the battle of Cuil.

*   *   *   *   *

Three objects I have left, the dearest to me
    On this peopled world :
Durrow, Derry, the noble angelic land,
    And Tir Luighdech,[1]
I have loved Erin's land of cascades,
    All but its government."[2]

On the day of Pentecost, 13th May, 563,[3] the exiled strife-monger, with guilt heavy on his soul and bitterness gnawing at his heart, landed on Iona, the "unknown island among the western waves"[4] upon which imperishable glory has been conferred by Columba's fame. The reasons which led him to choose this little island as the place of his exile have been set forth by the eighth Duke of Argyll, in his eloquent little book upon Iona, with words so luminous that I can do nothing better than quote them at length.[5]

"The causes which determined Columba in his selection of Iona are not mysterious. Some of them have been preserved in traditions which are as poetical as they are probably true ; whilst others are obvious on a moment's consideration of the position and of the character of the spot. In the first place it was an island ; and islands have been always popular with the monastic orders. They give seclusion, and with seclusion they afford facilities for the enforcement of discipline. Is it wrong to conjecture, also, that they

[1]For this place see Reeves, *Adamnan*, 1874, p. 232.

[2]Reeves, *Adamnan*, 1857, p. 275. Columba was certainly not the last person who "has loved Erin's land of cascades—all but its government !"

[3]For the chronology see Anderson, *Early Sources*, Vol. I., p. 43, note 2.

[4]Dr. Joseph Robertson on "Scottish Abbeys and Cathedrals," reprinted, 1891, from *Quarterly Review*, June 1849, p. 62.

[5]*Iona*, by the Duke of Argyll, IVth ed., pp. 76-83, 92-4. For a sketch map of Iona, and a plan showing the monastic sites, see Fig. 2.

satisfy that sense of possession which lies deep in human nature, and which has made even hermits rejoice in some rock which they could call their own? And then comes that ground of preference which has lived in the memory of the place for thirteen hundred years, and which must be true, for it stands in unmistakable harmony with the earlier events of Columba's life, and with a natural character which was full of strong and fierce emotions. He had been the cause—and by no means the innocent cause— of war and bloodshed in his native land. It was the censures of the Church and the contrition of his own soul which drove him into exile, and to the undertaking of some great labour in the cause of Christ. But the passionate love of an Irish Celt for his native Ireland seems to have burned in him with all the strength which is part of a powerful character. It is most true to nature—that which is related in the memories of his race—that he could not bear to live out of Ireland and yet within sight of her shores. On his voyage northwards in his boat of hides, he must have passed many islands—Islay first, but that probably was too large and too near—Jura next, but this also was no place for a hermitage, and the rocks of Antrim were still too close at hand.[1] Colonsay, with its little outlying islet, Oronsay—here was an island of the fitting size. Columba landed;[2] but on his ascending the heights, the blue land of Erin was still above the sea. On then, northwards, once more; and, as the same old poem represents him saying—

> ' My vision o'er the brine I stretch
> From the ample oaken planks;
> Large is the tear of my soft grey eye
> When I look back upon Erin.' [3]

The next land he touched was the land which he has made his own. If he landed, as no doubt he did, at the spot which continuous tradition has pointed out, he cannot have known, or he must have missed, the entrance to the Sound. Passing through a labyrinth of rocks, his boat was received into a creek which to this day retains the name of the Port of the Coracle (*Port-na-Churaich*)—a port guarded round by precipitous rocks of gneiss, and marked by a beach of brilliantly coloured pebbles of green serpentine, green quartz, and the reddest felspar. Again he mounted the nearest hill, and here at last the southern horizon was nothing but a line of sea. And so this hill has ever since been marked by a cairn which is known to the Gael as *'Cairn-cul-ri-*

[1] On Islay there still exist two church sites named Kilcholmkill (see *infra*, p. 67), but no foundation bearing his name appears to exist on Jura.

[2] For a discussion of Columba's presence on these islands see S. Grieve, *The Book of Colonsay and Oronsay*, vol. II., chap. vii.

[3] See the translation of this beautiful poem in Reeves, *Adamnan*, 1857, pp. 285-9.

B

Erin,' or the 'Cairn with the back turned upon Erin.'[1] Farther exploration must soon have discovered to Columba that the island on which he had now landed had other and more substantial recommendations. On the eastern side was the channel which he had missed, giving much-needed shelter from prevailing winds. Above all it was a fertile island, giving promise of ample sustenance for man and beast. It is true Iona is a rocky island, the bones protruding at frequent intervals through the skin of turf. Even there, however, Columba must have seen that the pasture was close and good; and not far from the spot on which he first swept the southern sky, he must have found that the heathy and rocky hills subsided into a lower tract, green with that delicious turf which, full of thyme and wild clovers, gathers upon soils of shelly sand. This tract is called in Gaelic ' The Machar ' or Sandy Plain. A little farther on, he must soon have found that the eastern or sheltered side presented a slope of fertile soil exactly suiting the essential conditions of ancient husbandry. At a time when artificial drainage was unknown, and in a rainy climate, the flats and hollows which in the Highlands are now generally the most valuable portions of the land, were occupied by swamps and moss. On the steep slopes alone, which afforded natural drainage, was it possible to raise cereal crops. . . . In the eastern slopes of Iona Columba and his companions found one tract of land which was as admirably adapted for the growth of corn as the remainder of it was suited to the support of flocks and herds. On the north-eastern side of the island, between the rocky pasturage and the shore, there is a long, natural declivity of arable soil steep enough to be naturally dry, and protected by the hill from the western blast. . . . The island now[2] supports upwards of 200 cows and heifers, 140 younger 'beasts,' about 600 sheep and lambs, 25 horses, and some three score of the pachyderms so dear to all the children of Erin. It grows also a considerable quantity of grain. But even these resources, ample as they might seem to be, were not enough for the growing number of the Columban monastery. Very soon

---

[1]On the other hand it has been pointed out that there are more instances of this name in the Isles. There is a *Cairn-cul-ri-Erin* in Oronsay—which of course might have originated in the same way as the cairn similarly called on Iona; for Columba, as stated in the text, is said to have landed on Oronsay before reaching his final destination. But on the island of Mull are *Carn-cul-ri-Erin* and *Carn-cul-ri-Alban*. This fact has led to the theory that these cairns marked the ancient boundary between Pictland and Dalriada. See Skene, *Celtic Scotland*, vol. I., p. 228, note. In that case Iona would presumably have been divided between the two states. This, of course, would quite accord with the respective statements of Tigernach and Bede, which bear that the Scotic and Pictish rulers both were concerned in the gift of the island to Columba. But the division of so small an island is improbable: and, having regard to the political situation, it is more likely, as pointed out hereafter, that the King of Dalriada made the gift and his Pictish overlord confirmed it. (For these cairns see also S. Grieve, *The Book of Colonsay and Oronsay*, vol. I., pp. 110-7.)

[2]That is, when the Duke of Argyll wrote. The first edition was published in 1870.

royal grants of neighbouring islands[1] made them tributary to the sustenance
of the Abbot and his brethren, and foremost among these came the productive
corn-bearing soil and the rich pastures of Tiree.   Fish were abundant, and
could be obtained at all seasons.   The large flounders of the Sound of Iona
are still an important item in the diet of its people.   The rocks and islets
all round swarmed with seals, and their flesh seems to have been a favourite
article of food.[2]   Their oil, also, doubtless supplied the light with which,
during many long winter evenings, Columba pored over his manuscripts of
the sacred text, or performed midnight services before the altar.''

We may readily picture Columba's little community,[3] with its
group of wooden or wattle huts floored with beaten earth ; its two barns,
stable, and byre ; its mill, its bakery, its kiln for corn-drying ; its
refectory for the common meal, its guest-house,[4] and its little heather-
thatched church of logs, with a sacristy opening on one side, where the
monastic bell was kept.[5]   Somewhat apart from the rest stood the Abbot's
house on rising ground, and the whole establishment was enclosed by
a fencible dry-built wall and earthen bank, and surrounded by the neat
patches of cultivated soil upon which the holy brethren worked.   Most
of them would be laymen, exempt from the heavy duties of religious
service, and wholly taken up with the practical work and manual labour
of the community.   The religious brethren, or monks proper, were
grouped into three classes—the Seniors, who were old men past active

[1]According to the *Annals of Tigernach* (ed. Whitley Stokes in *Revue Celtique*, Vol.
XVII, p. 151), Iona itself was made available to Columba by the gift of Conall MacComgall,
King of Dalriada.   On the other hand, Bede, *Ecclesiastical History*, Bk. III., ch. iv. (ed.
C. Plummer, vol. I., p. 133), says Columba received possession of the island from the Picts.
Probably the Pictish King, Brude MacMaelchon, who, after defeating the Scots in 560,
exercised the overlordship of Dalriada, confirmed a gift made in the first instance by Conall.
See a discussion of the question in Reeves, *Adamnan*, 1857, pp. 435-6: also in Skene, *Celtic
Scotland*, Vol. II., pp. 86-8, and *Chronicles of the Picts and Scots*, Preface, p. cxi.

[2] The monks of Iona had a seal-farm, either on the island of Soa, a mile and a half
to the south of Iona (E. C. Trenholme, *Story of Iona*, p. 31), or on the island of Erraid,
which is two miles to the south-east of Iona, close in to the Ross of Mull (Reeves, *Adamnan*,
1874, pp. cxlvi. and 262).   For the use of seals as food see Reeves, *Adamnan*, 1857, p. 78,
note g : and *cf.* S. Grieve, *The Book of Colonsay and Oronsay*, Vol. II, p. 222, note 1.

[3]For the site of the Columban monastery see Appendix I., p. 55.

[4] How high the Christian duty of hospitality was rated at Iona is illustrated by an
interesting story from Adamnan (Bk. I., ch. xxvi.) which shows how even a fast day might
be broken on the occasion of the arrival of a distinguished stranger.   So also the fierce curse
pronounced by Columba on a rich man who out of niggardliness refused to entertain him
(*ibid.*, Bk. II., ch. xx.).

[5]For a specimen of such bells see Fig. 37.

work and rich in holiness; the Working Brethren, on whom the main burden of the missionary and educational work of the monastery was cast; and the Juniors, or novices under instruction. The dress of the monks was of the simplest form. It consisted of a shirt of undyed wool reaching to the heels, and an upper garment with hood and sleeves; sandals of hide; and a white surplice for use at festivals. All classes lived with the greatest austerity, sleeping in their clothes on boards covered with straw.[1] "He never wore linen or wool next his skin," says the Old Irish Life of Columba. "He slept not except with his side against the bare earth, with nothing under his head but a pillar of stone for a pillow.[2] And he slept not at all, except for the time that his disciple Diarmait chanted three chapters of the *Beatus*. After that he rose up, and made lamentation and hand-clapping like a loving mother weeping for her only son. After that he sang the hundred and fifty psalms until morning, lying in the sand of the shore, as the poet said:

> ' The three fifties, heavy was the vigil;
> In the night, the torment was great.
> In the sea by the side of Alba, before the sun had risen,
> Bare he laid himself, noble afflictions,
> In the sand, great was the affliction.
> The course of his ribs was plain through his clothing,
> When the wind blew it.' " [3]

Any rational estimate of Columba's work as a cleric and a statesman must be guided by a thorough appreciation of the political circumstances

---

[1] An elaborate and highly interesting account of the constitution, discipline, and economy of the Columban settlement was compiled by Dr. Reeves from incidental references throughout Adamnan's *Life* (ed. 1874, pp. c.-cxxvii.). Our knowledge of the material condition of an early Celtic monastery has been enormously widened in quite recent years through the systematic excavations carried out at Nendrum (Mahee Island in Strangford Lough) by the Belfast Natural History and Philosophical Society. See *The Monastery of St. Mochaoi of Nendrum*, by H. C. Lawlor—a work of cardinal importance and absorbing interest to all students of the Celtic Church.

[2] For "St. Columba's Pillow" see Fig. 5, and *cf. infra*, p. 49.

[3] From the *Old Irish Life of St. Columba*, transl. Anderson, *Early Sources*, Vol. I, pp. 29-30. I have preferred to keep the original word Alba, rather than use the modern co-equivalent, Scotland, which has a very different meaning from the Kingdom of the Scots in Columba's time.

of his time;[1] and it is just in this essential matter that modern writers have so consistently been at fault.[2] When St. Ninian, the apostle of the Picts, began his great mission about the year 400—that is, over a century and a half before Columba's settlement on Iona—the Roman "Diocese of the Britains" yet stood, with its northern boundary, still nominally at least, at Hadrian's Wall.[3] Beyond that frontier line the whole of what we now call Scotland was inhabited by Celtic tribes whom the Romans, superbly contemptuous of racial complexities among the despised "barbarians," lumped together under the name of Picts.[4] At the end of the fifth century this native Pictish population began to be encroached upon from two sides. On the west, the immigration of Columba's countrymen, the Dalriad Scots from northern Ireland, led to the formation of the Kingdom of Dalriada, corresponding roughly to the modern Argyllshire, with the adjacent islands. Its political capital was the hill fort of Dunadd, in the Moss of Crinan;[5] and from 563 onwards its religious centre was at Iona, where St. Columba established his monastery. On the other side of Pictland the Angles, faring forth in

[1] See Map, Fig. 6.

[2] From the looseness of expression that has so strangely cursed many writers on Columba even Skene was not exempt. In his *Celtic Scotland*, vol. II., p. 93, he expatiates on the church of Iona, "which not only for a time embraced within its fold the whole of Scotland north of the Firths of Forth and Clyde, and was for a century and a half the national Church of Scotland, but was destined to give to the Angles of Northumbria the same form of Christianity for a period of thirty years." Even were the territorial radius of Iona's influence as wide as Skene imagined, no Scottish nation existed then or for centuries afterwards: to talk of the "national Church of Scotland" any time before the twelfth century, at the earliest, is simply absurd.

[3] See Appendix II., p. 56.

[4] For a recent discussion on the Picts see Professor W. J. Watson's paper in *Transactions of the Gaelic Society of Inverness*, vol. xxx., pp. 240-61.

[5] "The position of Dunadd as the capital of the lengthy, straggling Kingdom of Dalriada was not ill-chosen, being at the junction of the two sub-provinces of Lorn and Kintyre, the latter of which at that time extended as far north as the Crinan Loch; but it was rather open to attack by a force landing at Lochgilphead, which in a two hours' march could reach it by a route offering no physical difficulties. It is true, three forts, if they were contemporary, had to be passed on the way—Dunmore at Lochgilphead itself, Dunnamaraig near Cairnbaan, and Dunamuck—but these could only hold such small garrisons that, according to our modern ideas, they could easily be masked by a force operating against Dunadd, if they could not be at once stormed. . . . The channel of the Add, which flows close by on the north, is sunk several feet below the moss, which is here only 14 feet above the sea, so that possibly the river may have been navigable for small vessels of old, as far as Dunadd, where the effect of the tides, indeed, is still felt, although the sea is two miles distant in a straight line"—Dr. D. Christison in *Proc. Soc. Ant. Scot.*, Vol. XXXVIII, p. 226.

their white-winged war vessels over the tumbling waters from their timbered homesteads amid the flats and stanks of distant Denmark, poured into the Roman diocese now deserted by the legions, spread northwards and westward along the Firth of Forth, and occupied or reduced[1] the coastal area as far as the Pentlands. To this district they gave the name Bernicia. It formed the northern portion of the Anglian Kingdom of Northumbria, whose capital was the mighty rock of Bamborough, upon which in 547 King Ida planted his thorn-girt citadel. Lastly, driven westward before the tremendous weight of the Anglian inrush, the Roman Britons overflowed beyond the Solway, and spread as a refugee population northwards into and down the valley of the Clyde, forming the Britonic Kingdom of Strathclyde, with its capital on the rock of Alclyde, still known to-day as Dumbarton, the *dun* or fort of the Britons. So doing, this intrusive Britonic population elbowed aside a remnant of the original Pictish inhabitants, who retained their racial identity as the "Picts of Galloway" until the early thirteenth century.[2] The rest of Alba, beyond the Forth and Clyde, remained in

---

[1] The absence of pagan Anglian cemeteries in the Lothians suggests that the early Anglian occupation of Bernicia was a matter of domination rather than intrusion, and that the native Celtic population remained largely undisturbed. " It may be inferred that up to the time when Northumbria became Christian, in the first third of the seventh century, no permanent settlement of Angles had been made between the Tweed and the Forth."— *Ancient Monuments Commission, Report on East Lothian*, p. xiv.

[2] Mr. R. G. Collingwood, *Roman Britain*, pp. 99-100, argues against any great displacement of the provincial population owing to the Teutonic conquest. "One is tempted to fancy that the Celts who in Wales forgot their Roman culture were refugees from the south-east, civilised Romano-Britons driven from their homes by the Saxon invaders. But that is more than doubtful. The fully Romanised Britons were not driven into Wales and Cornwall by invaders from the east, they were caught between the eastern invaders and the western and destroyed where they stood. . . . The facts probably are that the Romanised part of Britain was harried to such an extent that its civilisation was wiped clean out; and that the Welsh and Cornish, who to some extent survived, survived precisely because, not being civilised, they were not worth harrying. The distribution of Celtic-speaking peoples in the early Anglo-Saxon period depends not on the pushing of Romanised Britons out of their homes but on their extinction, and the survival only of the non-Romanised in the west and north." While there may be an element of truth in this view, I should like to see the evidence. If Roman towns like Wroxeter were stormed and burned, others like Silchester have clearly been peacefully abandoned by their inhabitants, who presumably would have retired westward before the invaders advancing up the Thames. So also not all the villas that have been excavated show traces of violent destruction. In any case, whatever the evidence further south, it seems quite clear that there was a considerable displacement of population in the Solway-Clyde area. Only thus can we account for the formation of the Britonic Kingdom of Strathclyde and the survival of the Pictish remnant in Galloway.

the possession of the Picts. The capital of the Pictish confederation varied with the *locus* of the ruling King paramount: in Columba's time the sovereign was Brude MacMaelchon (*circa* 555-84), *rex potentissimus*,[1] who had his seat at Inverness.[2]

In my former work[3] I called attention to the entirely erroneous view, still widely held, that the Picts of Columba's day were utterly uncivilised—"savage clans and roving barbarians," as Dr. Johnson styled them.[4] Equally unjust is such an opinion about Columba's countrymen. It is indeed self-evident that the early Scotic immigrants must have shared in that brilliant civilisation which distinguished their mother-country, Ireland, in the later Iron Age and in early Christian times.[5] Fortunately a gleam of light is shed upon their domestic condition as the result of excavations undertaken in 1904-5 by the Society of Antiquaries of Scotland at Dunadd.[6] This interesting hill-fort, as we have seen, was the first capital of the Scots in Scotland, and therefore a short account of its excavation will not be out of place, both from the importance of the site and also by reason of the information thus available as to the cultural condition of the early Scots, to whom Columba ministered.

Dunadd has been well compared to the rock of Dumbarton, the capital of the Strathclyde Britons. Rising abruptly from the wide level

---

[1] Bede, *Ecclesiastical History*, Bk. III., ch. 4 (ed. C. Plummer, Vol. I., p. 133).

[2] Notwithstanding the doubts hinted by A. O. Anderson, *Early Sources*, Vol. I., p. 49, note 3, there seems no valid reason to reject the identification of Brude's capital with Inverness, first proposed by Dr. Reeves (*Adamnan*, 1874, p. 277). It seems to be clearly indicated in Adamnan's text. Two possible sites exist: the vitrified fort at Craig Phadrick, which Reeves favoured, and the entrenched ridge of Torvean, which was suggested by Skene (*Celtic Scotland*, vol. II., p. 106, footnote).

[3] *The Origins of Christianity in Aberdeenshire*, pp. 2-4. In the illustrations given in that work to show Pictish culture in Aberdeenshire, the vessels shown in Fig. 4 (p. 41), from Loch Kinnord and the Loch of Leys, should not have been included, as they are relics of the medieval castles there, not of the Pictish crannogs.

[4] *A Journey to the Western Islands of Scotland in 1773*, ed. D. T. Holmes, p. 218.

[5] Yet Mr. R. G. Collingwood (*Roman Britain*, p. 68) allows himself to speak of "naked Goidelic raiders." Historians of the later Roman Empire have in general underestimated the civilisation of its barbarian foes. Of the invaders of Britain the Angles and the Saxons were undoubtedly the most barbaric, yet they also were by no means devoid of a certain civilisation, as their cemeteries show.

[6] See the full report in *Proc. Soc. Ant. Scot.*, Vol. XXXIX., pp. 292-322.

Moss of Crinan, it culminates in twin tops,[1] of which the northern one is conical, while the other is a hog-backed ridge, forming the summit of the hill, 160 feet above the moor. On the east flank of the hill, immediately below the summit, is a broad sloping plateau. Advantage was taken of this configuration to form five main enclosures,[2] three on the ridge and two on the plateau : the northern peak was left unoccupied. The outer enclosure on the plateau was further sub-divided into two compartments. The walls screening all these divisions are carefully built without mortar, averaging about twelve feet thick.[3] At the north-east corner of the plateau is a cistern, and a flight of steps cut in the cliff leads up to the enclosures on the summit. Carved in the rock beside these steps are a human footprint, a cup-like depression 10 inches in diameter, and the well-executed figure of a boar, which have been thought to be connected with the investiture ceremony of the Kings of Dalriada.[4] The total area of the fort is about 220 feet square, much of which of course is uninhabitable. Dr. Christison, who conducted the excavations, estimated that it was capable of containing a population of about 700, but there was probably also a settlement outside the walls. The abundance of deep black soil found in the excavations led him to believe that sods were used in the construction of the inner buildings.

The number of relics recovered was large, and they throw a useful light upon the economy of the primitive Scotic capital. The agricultural life of the little community is vouched for by the presence of about fifty querns, all of the rotary pattern except three saddle querns.[5] Their handicrafts were varied, as shown by the large quantities of whet-stones and polishers, by hammer stones and pounders, by a grindstone, by stone moulds for casting rings and other objects, and by six crucibles in clay, two of which still showed traces of adhering bronze. Some of the domestic pottery was not wheel made, but most was skilfully turned, and two pieces were of salt-glazed ware. Nor was artistic capacity

[1]Fig. 7. The dominating character of the site is shown by the view (Fig. 10) looking outwards through the main entrance.

[2]See plan, Fig. 8.

[3]Fig. 9.

[4]See *Proc. Soc. Ant. Scot.*, Vol. XIII., pp. 28-47. The boar is shown at Fig. 11.

[5]Fig. 12. For other relics from Dunadd see Fig. 13.

lacking among the inhabitants of Dunadd. A piece of slate shows the well-executed, unfinished working drawing for a Celtic penannular brooch of attractive design, while on a second piece is scratched a pattern of scroll work and what seems to be a kind of cross. A clay mould for a simpler form of penannular brooch was also found. Another work of art was a carved stone ball of a kind usually restricted to sites within the limits of ancient Pictland. Fragments of jet ornaments were found, showing every stage in their manufacture on the spot, from the crude lump with the design drawn in outline to the finished bracelet. Two elegant bronze pins were also discovered, and a well-finished comb with artistic ornamentation. The list of personal ornaments is completed by a number of beads in blue or green glass, one with a pretty design of white stripes. The iron articles were numerous, including carding-combs, rings, knife-blades (one still with its wooden handle) and some eight or ten spear-blades. These last were the only weapons found, and the general picture suggested by the relics is that of a domestic community rather than a garrison. Evidence of Christianity is seen in a cross incised on one of the querns,[1] and also in a disc inscribed *"in nómine"* in Irish minuscules.[2] Brief and imperfect as it is, this glimpse at the life in old Dunadd is almost the only direct material evidence we yet possess as to the social condition and daily routine of Columba's countrymen.

Now of the four peoples—Scots, Angles, Britons, Picts—who struggled for mastery in what is now Scotland, the Angles alone were entirely outwith the pale of Christianity. They were thorough-going pagans, worshippers of Thor and Odin, pitilessly hostile to Christians wherever they found them. The Scots of Dalriada, coming from Ireland, shared in the more or less general acceptance of Christianity that had followed the mission of St. Patrick to that island in the earlier half of

---

[1]At Nendrum also a quern was found inscribed with a cross in relief—Lawlor, *op. cit.*, pp. 18, 137.

[2]The style of this inscription (see Fig. 13, No. 15) would suggest a date about the ninth century. The last recorded event in the history of Dunadd was its capture by the Pictish King Angus I MacFergus in 736—*Annals of Tigernach*, ed. W. Stokes in *Revue Celtique*, Vol. XVII., p. 239. Probably the place would lose its importance after Kenneth MacAlpin's union of the two realms in 843, when the seat of power was transferred to Scone.

C

the fifth century.[1]   The Britons of Strathclyde inherited the partial
Christianity of the Romanised provincials, of which St. Ninian's
mission itself had been an extension.[2]   During St. Columba's time the
leading Britonic churchman was St. Kentigern, who shortly before 567
planted his monastery at Cathures or Glasgow, where St. Ninian had
had a church before him,[3] and from this centre consolidated and revived
the struggling church of Strathclyde.   North of the Forth and Clyde
line the Picts, long before Columba's time, had received the Gospel
message from St. Ninian, who between the years 397 and 432 had conducted his great mission up the east coast probably as far as Shetland.
His work has been continued by other missionaries from his central community at *Candida Casa*, and by the local centres which they established,
such as those of St. Ternan at Banchory and St. Drostan at Deer.   The
evangelisation of the Picts was also carried on by Columba's contemporary Kentigern from Glasgow, who himself conducted a mission

---

[1]About 545, twenty years or thereby previous to Columba's settlement on Iona, St.
Brendan of Clonfert conducted a mission among the Dalriadic islands, founding churches
in Tiree, Bute, Seil, Culbrandan and (possibly) Elachnave in the Garvelloch Islands.   See
Skene, *Celtic Scotland*, vol. II., pp. 77-8.

[2] It is unfortunate that the evidence, literary and archæological, for Romano-British
Christianity is so meagre.   An authoritative statement may be found in Professor F. Haver-
field's *Roman Occupation of Britain*, revised by Sir G. **Macdonald**, p. 252, with references.
See also R. G. Collingwood, *Roman Britain*, pp. 95-6; but I cannot agree with the view
therein expressed that " the period [fourth century] when Christianity might have flourished
in Britain was a period of disaster and destruction when nothing could flourish."   It is
precisely in such periods that the Christian faith, with its unequalled message of consolation
to the suffering, flourishes most of all.   After all we must remember that it was just in this
very age, when the Roman power in the west was tottering to its ruin, that Christianity
obtained its greatest extension in the Empire, and overcame the last vestiges of a lingering
paganism, an outworn creed that had no message for those who were confronted with the
awful spectacle of a dying world.   In an age of unequalled suffering, where the pagan grimly
thought of Destiny, the Christian dwelt with unspeakable joy upon the Divine Message of
Consolation.   Also we have got to account for the historical fact that in the fifth and sixth
centuries, as epigraphic and literary evidence abundantly shows, the inhabitants of Wales
and Cornwall—descendants of the Roman provincials—were Christian.   The Teutonic conquest of Britain may indeed have destroyed the material remains of Romano-British
Christianity, but it is likely to have caused the extension rather than the obliteration of the
faith itself.

[3] See Joceline's *Life of St. Kentigern*, chap. ix. (ed. A. P. Forbes, p. 179).   In chapters
xxxix. and **xl.** (*ibid.*, pp. 229-32) Joceline gives an interesting account of a meeting between
Columba and Kentigern at Glasgow.   Certain details in this account, such as the mention
of large companies of singing clerics, and the exchange of pastoral staves by the two saints,
are quite unlike the practice of the medieval church, and were clearly derived by Joceline
from the old Celtic sources which he tells us in his Prologue that he used.

into Pictland that penetrated as far as central Aberdeenshire.[1]   Moreover, the work begun by Ninian was taken up, also in Columba's
lifetime, by the great monastery of the Irish Picts[2] founded in 558 by
St. Comgall the Great at Bangor in the Ards of Ulster (County Down).
St. Comgall himself, as we shall see, accompanied Columba on the
famous visit to the Pictish King Brude MacMaelchon at Inverness,
about which so much misunderstanding has arisen. His deputy, St.
Moluag, extended his missionary activities widely throughout Pictland,
ranging from Skye as far as Aberdeenshire, and even penetrated into
the hostile territory of the Scots in Dalriada.   About the very moment
when Columba landed on Iona, Moluag was establishing a community
of the Pictish church almost next door to him, on the island of Lismore.[3]
Both he and his master St. Comgall also founded churches in Tiree,
the granary of Iona.[4]   St. Moluag's other three chief monasteries were
planted, one at Rosemarkie in Easter Ross, the second at Mortlach on

---

[1] Joceline, doubtless drawing from his older sources, speaks of Kentigern in this mission
to Alba (*Albania*) "reclaiming that land from the worship of idols and *from profane rites
that were almost equal to idolatry*"—*prophanis ritibus ydolatrie pene equipollentibus* (*Life
of St. Kentigern*, ch. xxxiv., ed. A. P. Forbes, p. 220)—thus incidentally revealing that Pictland had already been partly Christianised.

[2] The Irish Picts (*Cruithne* or *Dal Araidhe*) were southern neighbours of the Scots
in Irish Dalriada. They inhabited Down and the southern part of Antrim. See Map, Fig. 1.

[3] The craze for ascribing all Christian work in Pictland to the Scotic Church of Iona
is well illustrated by Skene (*Celtic Scotland*, Vol. II., p. 133), who describes Moluag as a
disciple of Columba, and elsewhere (p. 157) speaks of Lismore as being "subject to Iona."
The real relations between Columba and Moluag will be discussed later on (*infra*, pp. 40-1).

[4] The site of *Kilmoluag*, with *Crois a' Moluag*, is still preserved in the name of a farm
near the north-west corner of the island, but all trace of St. Comgall's church seems to be
forgotten. The story of his foundation in Tiree in 564 is told in the *Old Life of St. Comgall*
(*Vitae Sanctorum Hiberniae*, ed. C. Plummer, Vol. II., p. 11). St. Brendan of Clonfert also
planted a church on the island (*ibid.*, vol. I., p. 143). This was probably the oldest religious
foundation (*cf. supra*, p. 18, note 1). Other church sites in Tiree, associated with known
saints, are *Kilfinnian*, perhaps from Abbot Findchan, who according to Adamnan (Bk. I.
ch. xxxvi.) founded a monastery on the island; *Cladh-Odhrain*, "Oran's cemetery," from
St. Oran (see *infra*, p. 20, note 5); *Kilchennich*, evidently a foundation of St. Kenneth,
Columba's companion in the journey to King Brude; *Kilbride*, from St. Bride; and *Temple
Patrick*. The word temple, *teampull*, is used of a stone church (see Prof. D. Mackinnon in
Scotsman, 8th December, 1887, also G. Petrie, *Ecclesiastical Architecture of Ireland*, IInd
ed., pp. 143-53), and this is evidently a later foundation, *dedicated* to the apostle
of Ireland. Previous to about the eighth century, as is well known, Celtic churches were
not dedicated to saints in heaven, but bore usually the names of their founders. Dr. Reeves
(*Adamnan*, 1874, pp. 310-17) tabulates no less than thirteen religious sites on this interesting
island, and justly recalls Adamnan's observation: *in ceteris eiusdem insulae monasteriis.*"
To his list Mr. Erskine Beveridge (*Coll and Tiree*, pp. 156-7) adds another, *Caibael Thomais*,
evidently a medieval dedication, and a second, *Tir a' Chaibel*, of unknown association. He
also points out that Columba himself had a church at Kirkapol (*op. cit.* pp. 147-9). The
site at Soroby, with its ancient cross and monumental slabs, is probably the *Campus Lunge*
of Adamnan, the penitential establishment which Columba placed under his successor
Baithene. Near it is a little creek still known as *Port-na-Luinge.*

the Deveron,[1] and the third at Clova in the uplands of Kildrummy. From Bangor of the Irish Picts, also in Columba's time, came St. Blaan, who presided over the monastery founded by St. Catan at Kingarth in Bute,[2] and himself founded another monastery at Dunblane. In northern Pictland, towards the end of Columba's lifetime, St. Donnan was working from his monastery on the island of Eigg, over a field which extended as far east as Auchterless, and as far north as Helmsdale. Columba's own erstwhile teacher, St. Finbar of Moville, had also recently conducted a widely-ranging mission into Pictland, his most northerly station being apparently at Dornoch.[3] Finbar, we must remember, had been trained at *Candida Casa,* the mother church of the Picts, and in thus penetrating up the eastern coast he was only following the footsteps of its founder, St. Ninian. These particulars, and many others that might be given, show how entirely mistaken is the common assumption that the Picts in Columba's time were still sunk in paganism. On the contrary, Christianity was already widely extended among them :[4] and it was a Christianity quite independent of, and anterior in origin to, the Scotic church based on Iona. The Pictish church in fact was based upon three main centres, *Candida Casa* and Glasgow, both of the Britons, and Bangor of the Irish Picts; and none of these had any organic connection whatsoever with Iona. Even on Iona itself Columba's church was not the first Christian post, for we hear before his time of a college of seven bishops on the island, and it is recorded that on his landing he was met by two bishops, who tried to send him away.[5]

[1] For symbol stones at Rosemarkie and Mortlach, see Figs. 14-17.

[2] Kingarth, like St. Moluag's monastery at Lismore, is described by Skene (*Celtic Scotland,* Vol. II., pp. 133, 157) as "subject to Iona." The mode of thought is revealed by the phrase " churches founded during his [Columba's] life, and *no doubt in connection with him*" [my italics]. It is upon such a gratuitous assumption, repeated until it has usurped the weight of a fact, that current modern conceptions of Columba's influence are largely based. For the remains of the Celtic monastery at Kingarth, see *Proc. Soc. Ant. Scot.,* Vol. XXXIV., pp. 307-25.

[3] The Rev. A. B. Scott (*Trans. Gael. Soc. Inverness,* Vol. XXVII., p. 22) claims that St. Finbar had also a church at Berriedale, but the evidence does not seem conclusive.

[4] The earliest Pictish King who there is some reason to believe was a Christian seems to be Nechtan Morbet (456-480). See Anderson, *Early Sources,* Vol. I., pp. cxx-i, and 122.

[5] See the *Old Irish Life* in Skene, *Celtic Scotland,* Vol. II, p. 491, also *ibid.,* pp. 34, 88; and in Anderson's *Early Sources,* vol. I., p. 45. The earliest kings of Dalriada, down to Gabhran MacDomongart (died 560) were buried in Iona, which argues the presence of a

intrusion[1] was a civil war among the Scots. The whole Clan Comgall rose in arms, and on their side Clan Gabhran mustered in support of Columba's nominee. At Delgu or Telocho,[2] somewhere in Kintyre, the opposing factions met, in the year 574: Duncan MacConall, the late King's son, was killed in the battle, and Aidan obtained a complete victory.[3] Thus for the second time Columba's passion for political intrigue had resulted in civil strife and bloodshed.

Aidan the False (574-606) proved himself a capable and vigorous ruler, and with Columba at his back he did much towards restoring the almost desperate fortunes of the Scots. "He exchanged the rank of a *toisech,* or Lord, for that of a *rig,* or King, and under him it was that the real foundation of the Scottish Monarchy was laid."[4] By land and sea he appears to have carried on a systematic policy of aggression against the Picts. Thus in 580 we find him attacking Brude MacMael-chon's kingdom in the rear by a descent upon the Orkneys; and ten years later he turned his arms against the Miathi, a southern tribe of the Pictish Confederation, who inhabited what is now Clackmannan-shire: Dumyat, the *dun* or fortress of the Miathi, a well-known summit

---

[1]Mr. J. Gavin Tait, writing in *Aberdeen Press and Journal,* 1st February, 1926, objects to this word. "As Aidan was the son of a former king, and as such undoubtedly eligible to succeed, I do not understand in what sense he is said to have been intruded." But it is clear from Adamnan's account that he was not the favoured candidate, and that his appointment was due to Columba's intervention. In any case, it was no business of the Abbot of Iona to dictate the occupancy of the Dalriadic throne. In a second letter (5th February, 1926), Mr. Tait, admitting this, added that, "in view of Columba's reputation for sanctity, together with his own royal birth and his relationship to the kings of Dalriada, it was nothing surprising that the question should be referred to his decision." But we are nowhere told that anybody referred the question to his decision: on the contrary it is clear that the initiative came from Columba himself. I submit that on the evidence the word "intrusion" is thoroughly justified.

[2]*Annals of Tigernach,* ed. W. Stokes in *Revue Celtique,* Vol. XVII, p. 151. For the probable site of Delgu, see Skene, *Celtic Scotland,* Vol. I., p. 142, note 41, and Vol. II., p. 85, note 4.

[3]Mr. Tait in his first letter flatly rejects this interpretation of the battle of Delgu, which I owe to Mr. A. B. Scott (*The Pictish Nation,* p. 207). "There was no civil war among the Scots in 574," says Mr. Tait. But I adhere to my view about the battle. Tigernach speaks of the slaughter of "many of the allies of the sons of Gabhran," and this language distinctly indicates party strife, Clan Gabhran being one of the three divisions of Dalriada.

[4]Reeves, *Adamnan,* 1857, p. 436.

of the Ochils opposite Stirling, is thought to preserve their name.[1] In all these acts of aggression King Aidan enjoyed the hearty support of Columba, whom Adamnan describes as praying for his victory over the "barbarians" during the campaign against the Miathi.[2] As Samuel to Saul, so Columba stood towards his nominee, King Aidan, who throughout his reign was a persistent foe of the Picts. It was thus not without good reason that the author of the "Prophecy of St. Berchan" sang about Columba: "Woe to the Picts to whom he will go eastward; if they knew that which approaches them: nor will it be happy with

[1] About 583 Aidan also gained a victory at "Man" (Tigernach, *Annals* in *Revue Celtique*, Vol. xvii., p. 153). It has been thought that this was Manan on the Forth (the name still preserved in Slamannan and Clackmannan), but Anderson (*Early Sources*, vol. I., pp. 89-90) suggests the Isle of Man, and thinks that in any case it is not to be identified with the " battle of the Miathi " mentioned by Adamnan (Bk. I., chaps. viii. and ix.). Tigernach, *ut supra*, p. 158, also chronicles a victory of Aidan at Leithrig, and this likewise has been identified with the *bellum Miathorum*, but apparently on no substantial ground (Anderson, *op. cit.*, vol. I., p. 97).

[2] A rather petulant critic, the Rev. C. L. Broun, writing in the *Scottish Chronicle*, 5th June, 1925, objects to my quoting the " battle of the Miathi " as proof of Columba's hostility towards the Picts. He quotes Dr. Fowler, who says (*Adamnan*, p. 197) that " the Miathi or Meatae were a British tribe dwelling by the northern Roman *vallum*, the Caledonians being beyond them." But if we accept this equation with the Meatae of Dion Cassius, who dwelt outside the Antonine Wall, then they would fall within the bounds of the Pictish confederation as understood in post-Roman times. In Dion's day the name Pict is not yet used, and the term Briton is applied without racial content to any inhabitant of Britannia. It does not yet bear the localised significance of later days when four nations strove for mastery in Alba. Bede (*Ecclesiastical History*, Bk. I., chap. i.—Plummer's ed., vol. I., p. 13), distinctly speaks of Britain north of the Firth of Clyde belonging to the Picts. *Cf.* Skene, *Celtic Scotland*, Vol. I, p. 162, footnote: "the term *barbari* is applied by Adamnan both to Picts and Saxons, but the name Miathi seems to belong to the Picts."

Mr. Broun, in his anxiety to reduce the volcanic figure of Columba to a sort of abstract conception of immaculate saintship, thus continues: " Even if they [the Miathi] had been Picts, surely (*e.g.*) an English missionary might pray for the victory of his fellow-countrymen over Red Indian or Zulu warriors, and yet afterwards evangelise them." I do not wish to enter apropos of St. Columba into a discussion about Zulus and Red Indians; but I am bound to castigate the monstrous assumption that the Picts stood to Columba's countrymen in the status of African savages to Englishmen. That Mr. Broun should have made this observation, in the course of a *critique* upon my *Origins of Christianity in Aberdeenshire*, in which the high civilisation of the Picts is set forth with archæological evidence, supplies another proof of how hopeless is the endeavour to eradicate the popular conception of the Picts as a race of naked, shivering barbarians.

In Adamnan, Bk. I., chap. vii., Columba is represented as prophesying the victory "granted by the Lord" to his kinsmen, the northern Hy-Neill, over the Irish Picts at Ondemone, somewhere near Coleraine, in 563.

him that an Irishman should be king in the east under the Picts."[1]   Yet this is the man to whom after generations have ascribed the conversion of Pictland!

With these facts in our minds, it becomes instructive to go back from the vague generalities of modern writers on Columba[2] to the authentic information supplied by his ancient biographer, Adamnan.   The modern writers, blissfully leaving out of account any consideration of the political circumstances of the time, describe him as wandering incessantly over the whole length and breadth of Scotland, mainland and islands included, founding churches almost literally from Maidenkirk to John o' Groat's, and from Buchan Ness to the Outer Hebrides.   But apart from the impossibility of one man covering such a field in one lifetime, as well as managing his monastic settlement at Iona,[3] there is no hint of these ceaseless peregrinations in Adamnan.[4]   In addition to the famous visits to King Brude MacMaelchon at Inverness, of which

[1]Berchan's Prophecy in Skene, *Chronicles of the Picts and Scots*, p. 82.   It is right to say that at this point the text does not make it quite clear whether the reference is to Columba himself or to Aidan.   But in any case their policy was the same.   Mr. Tait, being confronted with this little piece of evidence as to the true nature of Scoto-Pictish relations, remarks superfluously (*Aberdeen Press and Journal*, 5th February, 1926): "The prophecy is put into Berchan's mouth as a prediction of future events, but is really a prophecy after the event."   I do not imagine that any of my readers are in danger of accepting the " Prophecy of St. Berchan" as a genuine piece of divine revelation: my point is simply that the phrase put into the prophet's mouth accurately reflects the political situation as the compiler of the prophecy understood it.

[2]As an example of these may be instanced the recent work of Miss Lucy Menzies on *St. Columba of Iona*.   I mention it not by any means to disparage an altogether charming book, which mirrors the very spirit of Iona and the Western Isles, and the reading of which has afforded me a deal of pleasure.   But the book, while containing much useful information, makes no real attempt to face the facts and form some conclusion as to the actual nature and scope of Columba's work in relation to his political environment.

[3]After all, as Mr. A. O. Anderson writes to me, Columba "was an abbot, not a missionary, and as abbot was more or less tied to his monastery."

[4]It is highly significant that Bede, in describing the numerous monasteries afterwards included in the Columban Order, mentions only Derry and Iona as actual foundations of Columba in person, and expressly states that the others were subsequently " multiplied by his followers " from these two centres: *ex quo utroque monasterio plurima exinde monasteria per discipulos eius et in Britannia et in Hibernia propagata sunt*—Eccles. Hist., Bk. III., chap. iv. (Plummer's ed., Vol. I., p. 134).   Recollection of the fact that any community subsequently founded from Iona would be styled one of Columba's monasteries, will save us from stressing unduly Adamnan's remark: "*sancto Columbae, cuius monasteria intra utrorum populorum [Pictorum et Scotorum] terminos fundata ab utrisque ad presens tempus valde sunt honorificata*"—Bk. II., Chap. XLVI.

D

two are chronicled,[1] Adamnan speaks on three occasions only of Columba as having been beyond the *dorsum Britanniae,* or central mountain ridge of Scotland (Drumalban): and as his arrangement is not chronological it is not certain that these were separate occasions. Elsewhere he speaks definitely of Columba as being only in Ardnamurchan, in Skye, in Kintyre, in Lochaber, possibly in Morven,[2] and on Loch Ness (no doubt on his journey to King Brude). And so far from Columba being the apostle of the Picts, Adamnan specifically records that on two occasions when he was conversing with men of this nation, he required the services of an interpreter![3] His relations with the Picts, as we have seen, were not apostolic but distinctly antagonistic: to him, as to his successor Adamnan, they were an inferior race, spoken of in terms of scorn, looked down upon as "gentiles" and "barbarians" or "barbarous heathen," terms repeatedly

[1]Dr. Fowler (*Adamnan*, p. 62) says that Columba "frequently visited" King Brude. This is just another example of the looseness of expression that seems to have overtaken so many writers on Columba. Following up the usual conception of Columba as a missionary ceaselessly perambulating the whole of North Britain, Dr. Fowler proceeds: "Sometimes, no doubt, he visited his monastery there [at Iona], for he retained the leadership as long as he lived, one of the brethren taking his place during his absences." But Adamnan's biography in no way justifies such a picture of Columba as a merely occasional visitor to Iona. On the contrary, it distinctly suggests that the Abbot was in fairly constant residence, and kept a close oversight over all that went on in the island. The journeyings are mentioned incidentally as exceptional occasions.

[2]If, as seems quite likely, *Coire Salchain*, in Bk. I., chap. XLVI., is Sallachan opposite Aros (Sallochanecorry in 1509—*Registrum Magni Sigilli Regum Scotorum*, 1424-1513, No. 3284). See Reeves, *Adamnan*, 1857, p. 88, note a; 1874, p. 264. But the name is a fairly common one.

[3]Much ink has already been spilt upon this question. Mr. Tait, *Aberdeen Press and Journal*, 1st February, 1926, follows the traditional line of explanation. "At the date of the two incidents mentioned by Adamnan Columba had evidently not acquired a sufficient knowledge of the Pictish language to be able to preach in it." But the point which all such argument ignores is that Adamnan's arrangement is not chronological, and, therefore, we have no evidence as to the periods in Columba's life when these incidents occurred. At the same time I do not wish to stress this point as to Columba requiring an interpreter, except in so far as it fits in with my general view of his scope and work. We must remember that there may have been many very different dialects in use among the Picts. Mr. Tait pointed out that St. Aidan, whom Iona sent to be the apostle of the Northumbrian Angles, required the services of King Oswald as interpreter. But the two cases are not parallel. Aidan's mission was conducted with the co-operation and under the authority of the Crown, whereas Columba, according to my view, did not enjoy the support of King Brude or the friendship of his subjects.

used in referring to them throughout Adamnan's Life. Even the much misunderstood journey to King Brude in 564 was probably a political rather than a religious mission, having for its object the rehabilitation of his Dalriadic kinsmen whom Brude in the recent campaign had so severely mishandled. Contrary to Bede and later writers who have followed him, Adamnan nowhere states that Columba converted Brude, he merely says that the Pictish King held him in high honour.[1] It has long been pointed out as a suspicious circumstance that no church foundation of Columba exists at Inverness.[2] We may be quite certain that had Brude accepted Christianity from Columba he would have allowed the saint to establish a church in his capital, and that a church connected with so memorable an event would not afterwards have been forgotten. Moreover, while Adamnan, anxious to exalt the glory of his predecessor, mentions Columba alone in describing the negotiations with King Brude, we know from the old Irish sources that he was accompanied on this occasion by two very eminent Pictish ecclesiastics, both old fellow-students of his own at Clonard and Glasnevin: St. Comgall the Great, founder and Abbot of Bangor of the Irish Picts, and St. Kenneth of Aghabo in Ossory, and of Kilrymont in Fife—the place afterwards called St. Andrews.[3] Scotic writers from Adamnan downwards have ascribed to Columba the whole credit of the visit to King Brude, ignoring entirely his two distinguished Pictish companions. In the old Life of St. Comgall, on the other hand, the journey is placed in its true perspective, Columba there receiving his fair share and no more

---

[1] Gartnaidh MacDomelch (584-599 or 601), Brude MacMaelchon's successor, certainly was a Christian. His territories were apparently in the Tay valley, and either he or his successor, Nechtan of the race of Verb, who died in 621, founded a church at Abernethy (Skene, *Chronicles of the Picts and Scots*, p. 150: *iste edificavit Abernethyn*). *Cf.* Anderson, *Early Sources*, vol. I., p. 121, note 3.

[2] The nearest church associated with Columba's name is at Petty. *Walterus vicarius Sancte Columbe de Petyn* is mentioned in the *Registrum Episcopatus Moraviensis*, p. 43, *circa* 1208-15. But it is doubtful whether this is not a *dedication* of the Roman period.

[3] St. Kenneth had a church and churchyard (*Cill Chainnich* and *Cladh Chainnich*) on Iona. The site is a little to the west of Maclean's Cross, between the village and *Releig Orain*, and close to the present Parish Church (see Map, Fig. 2). In the churchyard was found a pear-shaped stone, 1 foot 7 inches long, bearing an incised cross with expanded fantailed terminals to the head and arms. It is now preserved in the Cathedral, and is figured in Trenholme's *Iona*, plate 33.

of the credit for an undertaking in which he was not the sole or even the principal partner.[1]

A critical examination of Columba's work brings out most strongly the fact that his apostolic labours were almost entirely restricted to his Scotic fellow-nationals of Dalriada, with whom his sympathies were completely bound up, and to the Pictish tribes on the Dalriadic frontier who came under the influence of the intrusive and dominating race.[2] Even at his own doors we have seen how the Pictish St. Moluag was working independently of him, planting churches in Tiree, in Mull, in Skye, in Lewis, and elsewhere in the Western Islands. How far

[1] Adamnan merely mentions "companions," leaving it to be inferred that they were some of Columba's disciples. Skene, *Celtic Scotland*, Vol. II., p. 106, rightly comments upon the omission:—"Adamnan does not tell us who his companions were, which is unusual with him; but we learn from the *Life of St. Comgall* that they were, in point of fact, two of the most distinguished saints of the period—Comgall of Bangor and Cainnech of Achaboe. They both belonged to the race of the Irish Picts; and, therefore, Columba probably thought that his mission to the King of the Picts of Scotland would be materially aided by their presence." The motive for Adamnan's "unusual" silence is, of course, perfectly obvious.

[2] Columba's monastery at Lochcolumkille, in Kilmuir parish, Skye, seems to be an example of a foundation of the latter class: from Adamnan, Bk. I., ch. 33, it appears that in Columba's time Skye belonged to the Picts. Dr. Reeves has pointed out (*Adamnan*, 1874, p. 274) that Columba appears to have worked over the north-eastern part of the island, beyond a line drawn from Portree to Loch Snizort Beag; while the rest was evangelised from Bangor by St. Maelrubha, who settled at Abercrossan (Applecross) in 673, and was martyred on 21st April, 722. Even within the part specially connected with Columba, his Pictish rival, St. Moluag, planted a church at *Kilmoluag*, near the extreme north end of the island. Columba's foundation was on an island in Loch Columkille (now drained), and from Dr. Reeves' descriptive notes it must have been a very typical specimen of a Celtic monastery. *Cf.* also J. A. MacCulloch, *The Misty Isle of Skye*, 3rd ed., pp. 46-8, 277-8.

Further south, at Skeabost, is a church known in 1501 as "Sanct Colmez Kirk" (*Registrum Secreti Sigilli Regum Scotorum*, Vol. I, No. 675: *cf. Origines Parochiales Scotiae*, ed. C. Innes, Vol. II., part I., p. 355), which Dr. Reeves likewise connects with Columba. But we shall see that Columba's genuine foundations probably always bore the name Columkille; and the various church sites in Scotland known as St. Colm's are doubtless to be associated with some of the numerous saints bearing that name, such as the St. Colm who has been confused with St. Columba in Aberdeenshire. It is significant that the site at Skeabost is associated with a *Pictish* symbol-stone (see Fig. 18) of the kind typical of early church sites in Scotland beyond Drumalban, and not found within the confines of ancient Dalriada. These symbol-stones are almost unknown in the Western Isles. There is one at Benbecula (Fig. 19), and one at Pabbay, in St. Moluag's Churchyard (Figs. 20 and 21). Note again the association of the symbol-stone with a *Pictish* foundation. I have discussed the probable significance of the distribution of these symbol-stones in my *Origins of Christianity in Aberdeenshire*, pp. 9-11: see also the section on "The Archæological Evidence" in the present work (*infra*, pp. 73-8).

The Scotic occupation of Skye seems to have taken place in 668 and 670—see Tigernach, *Annals*, ed. W. Stokes in *Revue Celtique*, Vol. XVII., pp. 200-1.

Columba penetrated into Pictish territory it is of course difficult to tell. It seems fairly clear that his activities extended as far as the upper Tay—though the reception he got there is hinted by the words of his panegyrist, Dallan Forgaill, who boasted that the saint "shut the mouths of the fierce ones who dwelt with Tay's High King!"[1]   On another occasion when Columba was in Pictland a "rival" tried to destroy him by setting fire to a village in which he was thought to have lodged.[2] Possibly the extension of Columba's work in Strathtay may be connected with the early Scotic penetration of Gowrie, which Professor Watson has recently propounded: though on this latter question I must own grave doubts.   At Invermoriston on Loch Ness,[3] and at Kingussie in Strathspey, are church sites that may be undoubted Columban foundations: both, of course, lie on alternative routes which the Saint might

[1]In the *Amra Choluimbchille*, a eulogy written in gratitude for Columba's intervention on behalf of the bards at the Synod of Drumceatt in 574 (see *infra*, pp. 43-4); edited by W. Stokes in *Revue Celtique*, Vol. XX, p. 401. *Cf.* Anderson, *Early Sources*, Vol. I, p. 52, Note 2. Skene (*Celtic Scotland*, Vol. II., pp. 135-7) suggested that the extension of Columba's activities into Strathtay may have followed on the death of Brude MacMaelchon in 584, as his successor, Gartnaidh MacDomelch (584-601), who was certainly a Christian, seems to have had his royal seat at Abernethy.

If the Church of Drymen be accepted as a genuine Columban foundation, this indicates an expansion of Columba's influence not merely eastward towards the Tay, but also in a south-easterly direction on to the territory of the Strathclyde Britons. And if we adopt the view that this forward movement of the Iona Church dates from after King Gartnaidh's accession in 584, it becomes very significant to observe how this date coincides with the famous meeting between Columba and Kentigern. As Skene points out (*Celtic Scotland*, Vol. II., p. 194), this meeting cannot have taken place before *circa* 582, i.e., just about the time when Columba was developing missionary activity on the borders of Strathclyde and in the adjacent Pictish lands. We know (see *ante*, p. 18) that Kentigern on his part organised a mission which reached the uplands of Mar, and thus followed a line transversely to Columba's penetration. From these facts it is reasonable to assume that the meeting between the two great Saints took place with the purpose of demarcating their respective spheres of influence, and thus obviating the possibility of friction between the Iona and Strathclyde Churches. That some kind of bargain was struck may perhaps be inferred from the incident, preserved by Joceline (see *supra*, p. 18, note 3) of the exchange of pastoral staves between them.

It has been thought that Dunkeld was a foundation of St. Columba: but of this there is no evidence, and Dr. Reeves has shown (*Adamnan*, 1874, pp. lxix-lxx) that the name of the patron saint was almost certainly transferred thither after 849, when Kenneth MacAlpin made Dunkeld the head of the Columban Church in his united realm.

[2]Adamnan, Bk. I., ch. XXXIV.   Taken by itself, such an incident might not prove much: but it suggests an atmosphere, and fits into the general picture.

[3]Here is *Clachan Columchille*, with Columba's Well in the vicinity.   See Dr. W. Mackay, "Saints Associated with the Valley of the Ness," in *Trans. Gaelic Soc. Inverness*, Vol. XXVII., p. 151: reprinted in *Sidelights on Highland History*, p. 97.

have used in journeying to and from the Pictish capital at Inverness.[1] It is important to note that the churches ascribed to Columba within the confines and neighbourhood of ancient Dalriada, where his real work was done, are always known as *Kilcolumcille,* "the church of Columcille," preserving his true ancient designation, whereas this name is not found in the east coast churches ascribed to him—the names of which, such as St. Comb's and St. Colm's in Aberdeenshire, still reveal the true identity of the missionaries who founded them. This vital fact was realised as long ago as 1858 by Dr. George Petrie, who then wrote: "I suspect that all the churches founded by Columba bore anciently the name of Columbkill."[2]

Why the glory of Columba's name and the extent of his influence should have been so enormously exaggerated in after ages was implicit in the facts of subsequent history. Out of the long struggle between the Scots of Dalriada and their unwilling hosts, the Picts, it was the Scots who emerged triumphant. After the accession in 843 of Kenneth MacAlpin, King of Dalriada, half a Pict by blood but wholly a Scot by sympathy, to the combined throne of Dalriada and Pictland, the Scotic or Columban Church came first to dominate and thereafter to absorb its Brito-Pictish predecessor. And with the extension of the Scotic church extended also the glory of its founder and patron saint, Columba. Moreover, even before the event of 843 there are signs of weakening in the Pictish Church. About the year 730, its illustrious parent, St. Ninian's monastery at *Candida Casa,* was absorbed by the English of Northumbria, and forthwith was reorganised on Roman lines. "From being

---

[1] For these routes see Skene's notes in Reeves, *Adamnan,* 1874, p. 328. These church sites, with the doubtful one at Petty, are the only places connected with Columba anywhere near Inverness. Yet Dr. Fowler (*Adamnan,* p. 62), could write:—"The number of churches dedicated to St. Columba in that neighbourhood still bears witness to the mark which he made."

[2] See Sir J. Y. Simpson, *Archæological Essays,* Vol. I., p. 73. A correct view of the real scope of the Columban mission enables us, I think, to understand the much discussed *expulsio familie Ie trans Dorsum Britanniae* by the Pictish King Nechtan MacDerile in 717 (Tigernach, *Annals,* ed. W. Stokes in *Revue Celtique,* Vol. XVII, p. 225). This was certainly not a national "trek" from Pictland of the Columban clerics to whom the conversion of the whole country has been ascribed. If it was, who took their places? Did the Picts relapse into heathenism? So far as we can understand it, Nechtan's action was simply the ejection of certain intrusive settlements of Scotic clerics, against whom Pictish national sentiment and the jealousy of the Pictish church had been aroused.

the mother-church of the Britons and Picts it was degraded to be the church of a local diocese, subordinate to York."[1]   Thereafter the Pictish Church would be dependent on Bangor in Ulster; and probably as an inevitable consequence of its remoteness from the new headquarters we may trace throughout the eighth century a slow but steady weakening, which was materially hastened by the cruel struggle with the Vikings that began at this period.   The same century also witnessed the birth and rapid growth of the antagonism within the native church between those who favoured amalgamation with Rome and those who stood out for the ancient system.   The Romanists received a powerful impulse from the policy of King Nechtan MacDerile (706-24), and his ecclesiastical adviser Curitan (St. Boniface), who began the practice, which has led to such confusion among later medieval writers, of dedicating the old Celtic churches in accordance with the Roman hagiology. Nechtan introduced the *cultus* of St. Peter, and his successor Angus I. MacFergus (729-61), the greatest of all the sovereigns of Pictland, introduced that of St. Andrew, who later became the patron saint of the united realm.

The Pictish Church, thus weakened by isolation and by Roman influences, was injured beyond recovery by the Norse devastations: and, after the union of the two realms in 843, Kenneth MacAlpin began a policy of thorough-going reform, relying mainly upon Anglian and Scotic clergy who had conformed to the ways of Rome.   An important step in this direction was taken in 849 by the translation of St. Columba's relics, and the headquarters of the Romanised Scotic Church, from Iona to Dunkeld.[2]   Iona was terribly exposed to the

---

[1]Scott, *Pictish Nation*, p. 103.

[2]Just as Dunkeld succeeded Iona in the primacy in Scotland, so also Kells, not of great importance in Columba's time, became, in 814, the capital of his Order in Ireland.   The decline in importance of Iona in the ninth century is revealed by the appointment after 854 of a pluralist Abbot, Cellach MacAilill, who also held the presidency of Kildare—see *Annals of Ulster*, ed. W. M. Hennessy, Vol. I., p. 374.   (Kildare was not a Columban foundation.) Yet, Kenneth MacAlpin himself was buried in Iona in 858 (Skene, *Chronicles of the Picts and Scots*, p. 151); and for the next two centuries the island continued to be a highly favoured place of royal sepulture.   The last prince to be buried here seems to have been Lulach the Simpleton, stepson of Macbeth, who was slain at Essie, in Strathbogie, on 17th March, 1058. Curiously enough, Iona does not seem to have been a burial place of the Kings of Dalriada after Aidan the False.   According to Fordun (*Scotichronicon*, Bk. III., Ch. XXXVIII., ed. W. Goodall, Vol. I., pp. 144-5) Aidan was buried at Kilkerran, near Campbeltown, in

Viking raids,[1] and moreover was not in a sufficiently central position for the united kingdom over which Kenneth now ruled. Subsequently the ecclesiastical metropolis was shifted still further eastward to Abernethy, an old Pictish capital and religious centre. We have to this day a standing memorial of the arrival of the Scotic Church at Abernethy in the round tower[2] which is the justly celebrated feature of the quiet little town about which so many ancient memories cluster. The style of this type of ecclesiastical structure is purely Irish,[3] although the Romanesque details of its windows, and the character of its masonry, leave us in no doubt that the Abernethy tower in its present state is not older than the end of the eleventh century. Its twin[4] at Brechin, however, is completely Irish in all its features; and there can be no hesitation in ascribing its origin to the days of Kenneth II. MacMaelcoluim, who about 990 introduced Scotic clergy into this ancient Pictish centre— "gave to the Lord the great monastery of Brechin," as the Scoto-Roman monk expressed it from his point of view.[5] The presence of these two Irish towers in the very heart of old Pictland speaks to us in no uncertain voice about the triumph of the Scotic Church of Iona and the eclipse of its Brito-Pictish predecessor.

Kintyre: *apud Kilcheran, quo praedecessorum nullus antea, tumulatur*. This is said to have been the original seat of the Dalriadic monarchy before Dunadd. Kilkerran Church may possibly take its name from St. Ciaran, one of the "Twelve Apostles of Erin," founder and Abbot of Clonmacnoise, a friend of Columba, who died in 544 or 549 (see Fowler, *Adamnan*, pp. 48-9). Two fine Celtic cross-shafts of late design (about 1500), lying in the churchyard, are illustrated by Stuart, *Sculptured Stones of Scotland*, Vol. II., Plates LIV. and LV., and remind us of the long-descended distinction of the place.

[1] Iona was ravaged in 795, 802, 806, 825, 976 and 986.

[2] Fig. 22.

[3] There was apparently a round tower on Iona itself—see Champneys, *Irish Ecclesiastical Architecture*, p. xxxii. (note to p. 61): also Trenholme, *Iona*, p. 118.

[4] Figs. 23, 24. At Fig. 25 an Irish round tower is shown for comparison.

[5] "*Hic est qui tribuit magnam civitatem Brechne Domino*"—*Chronicles of the Picts and Scots*, ed. W. F. Skene, p. 10. *Civitas* is regularly used of a monastic community. In spite of the fact that he did not realise the distinction between the churches of the Picts and the Scots, Skene appears to have had a just perception of the significance of this action, for he writes (*Celtic Scotland*, Vol. II., p. 332) that "the object of King Kenneth in this foundation may have been to bring a Pictish population more under the direct influence of the Scots." So also *ibid.*, p. 400: "like the other churches which belong to the period after the establishment of the Scottish dynasty on the throne in the person of Kenneth MacAlpin, it emanated from the Irish Church, and was assimilated in its character to the Irish monasteries; and to this we may no doubt attribute the well-known round tower at Brechin."

Widely different on the other hand was the fortune of the Church that Columba founded. The shrewd political insight of its author seems to have stamped itself ineradicably upon the Church of Iona; and at a time when the Pictish Church still clung tenaciously to the old traditions, the religious leaders of the Scots found their account in aligning themselves with Rome, and thus with the future. This process of conformation began in the time of Adamnan, ninth Abbot of Iona (679-704), the biographer of Columba. After a visit to Northumbria in 686 he came back a convinced adherent of Roman observances. The abbot, however, failed immediately to persuade his brethren, and after his death there was a schism on the island, Columban and Roman parties forming under rival abbots.[1] The conformation of Iona with Rome was thus not completed until 767. While the Columban Church threw in its lot so early with Rome, the remnants of the Pictish Church remained dissident to the last, apparently as the Culdees of the twelfth and thirteenth centuries.[2] Hence all through the later Middle Ages the Roman Church writers misread or garbled the records of Celtic Christianity, ascribing to Columba and the Scotic school of Iona much of the work that was in fact performed by Ninian and Kentigern and their successors of the Brito-Pictish Church. A striking example of this occurs in the case of the famous monastery of Deer in Buchan; and

[1] For a table of the rival abbots see Skene, *Celtic Scotland*, Vol. II, p. 288, note 30.

[2] A glance at the map (Fig. 26) will show how the Culdee sites in Scotland group themselves along the eastern side of Drumalban—i.e., the area not served by the Columban Church. To this rule there are two apparent exceptions: Lismore, and Iona itself. But at Lismore the Pictish St. Moluag, a contemporary of St. Columba, had founded a monastery, *circa* 558-63. The evidence for Culdees at Iona rests on very late authority (*Annals of Ulster*, under date 1164), and they were merely a section of the religious community there, having their own head—see Reeves, "On the Céli-dé, commonly called Culdees," in *Transactions of the Royal Irish Academy*, Vol. XXIV., part III. (1873), p. 168-9. Perhaps the Culdee community here was descended from the conservative minority who had refused to accept the Roman discipline and observances, or even from the pre-Columban Christian community on the island.

It has been sometimes thought that the Culdee settlement at Monymusk was an Iona foundation, because of the association of this place with the Brecbannoch of St. Columba. But this famous reliquary (Fig. 27), now preserved at Monymusk House, has no ascertainable connection either with the Culdee College or with the later Priory of Augustinian Canons-regular. It was associated with the lands of Forglen, in Banffshire, and came into the hereditary wardenship of the manorial family of the De Monymusks in 1315. See my paper on "The Augustinian Priory and Parish Church of Monymusk" in *Proc. Soc. Ant. Scot.*, Vol. LIX., pp. 38-40.

E

owing to the fortunate circumstance that we are able here to some extent
to trace the process of garbling actually at work, it may be instructive
to examine the evidence and its interpretation in some little detail.

The traditional account of the foundation of the old Celtic monastery
at Deer, as believed by the monks inhabiting the place in the twelfth
century, is set forth in the famous Gaelic entry in the Book of Deer.[1]
This entry has been translated as follows :—

" Columcille and Drostan, son of Cosgrach, his pupil, came from I
as God had shown them unto Abbordoboir,[2] and Bede the Pict was mormaeor
of Buchan before them, and it was he that gave them that town in freedom
for ever from mormaeor and toshach.[3] They came after that to the other
town ; and it was pleasing to Columcille, because it was full of God's grace,
and he asked of the mormaeor, to wit Bede, that he should give it to him.
And he did not give it ; and a son of his took ill after refusing the clerics,
and he was nearly dead. After this the mormaeor went to intreat the
clerics that they should make prayer for the son, that health should come to
him ; and he gave in offering to them from *Cloch-in-tiprat* to *Cloch-pette-mic-
Garnait.*[4] They made the prayer, and health came to him. After that
Columcille gave to Drostan that town, and blessed it, and left as his word :—
'Whosoever should come against it, let him not be many-yeared or victorious.'
Drostan's tears came on parting with Columcille. Said Columcille, 'Let
Dear[5] be its name henceforward.' "

[1] The Book of Deer is a manuscript volume of 86 parchment folios, now preserved in
the University Library, Cambridge. It contains the complete Gospel of St. John and portions
of the other three Gospels, in a degraded version of the Vulgate, along with the Apostles'
Creed, a fragment of an Office for the Visitation of the Sick, a transcript of a charter by
David I., and a most interesting series of vernacular memoranda, dating from the eleventh
and twelfth centuries, written on the margins of the volume, and describing gifts and
immunities conferred upon the monastery mainly by Celtic chiefs of Buchan. The edition
I have used is that prepared by Dr. John Stuart for the Spalding Club in 1869. For other
editions see Anderson, *Early Sources*, Vol. I., pp. xxxvii-viii.

[2] Aberdour. It is a significant comment on the authenticity of the legend that,
although the legend says that Columba conferred only Deer upon Drostan, at Aberdour the
ancient church bears St. Drostan's name, and also contained his relics enshrined in a stone
chest—Forbes, *Kalendars of Scottish Saints*, p. 327. On the foreshore to the right of the
bay is St. Drostan's Well, and in the neighbourhood is Durstane's Slack. Subsequent
Roman influences are revealed by Mess John's Well to the left of the bay, and by Mary Den,
a side glen opening eastward from the Dour valley above Aberdour, with a well.

[3] i.e., freedom from control and exactions by the territorial magnates.

[4] These names may be translated as "the stone of the well," and "the stone of the
farm of Gartnaidh's son." These old boundary stones have long since perished, and the
locality of the grant is thus unknown.

[5] *deara*—a punning attempt to explain the meaning of the name Deer. The word
really means the place of oaks (*cf.* Derry). In the neighbourhood are Aikie Hill and Aikie
Brae.

Thus it will be seen that in the twelfth century the Celtic monks of Deer asserted that their community, situated on the north-eastern coast of old Pictland, had been founded by St. Columba, the apostle and champion of the Dalriadic Scots, and that its first abbot was St. Drostan, whom they represented as a disciple of St. Columba.

The first person, so far as I am aware, to hint a doubt as to the authenticity of this legendary account was Dr. John Hill Burton. Writing in 1873, with shrewd suspicion he pointed out that "there is no reference to the brotherhood of Deer in any of the ancient works about Columba." [1] He might also have added that the name of Drostan, which is a Pictish not a Scotic one,[2] does not appear in any of the older lists of Columba's disciples. Twelve years later, in 1885, Dr. Alexander Macbain made a searching analysis of what he boldly and truly called the "Myth of Deer," restoring St. Drostan to his true position as the founder of the monastery, and referring that event to its correct chronological horizon.[3] At the moment Dr. Macbain was concerned only with Deer, but it is evident from an incidental remark which he drops that he had arrived at a true general idea about the real position of Columba—who, he says in a remarkable passage, "swallowed up into his own fame all the work of his predecessors, companions, and contemporaries, and deprived generations of pioneers and missionaries of their just fame." Modern research has amply confirmed the view so courageously set forth by Dr. Macbain forty years ago. The Church of the Picts has now been restored to its true position as one of the most illustrious branches of the Celto-Catholic Church, independent of, and anterior in origin to, the Church of the Scots founded by St. Columba at Iona in 563.

When once the general historical position is realised, it becomes possible to approach the few authentic particulars about the historical St. Drostan[4] with some likelihood of obtaining a just understanding

[1] *History of Scotland*, 1873: ed. 1905, Vol. I., p. 410, note 1.

[2] See the reff. in index, Anderson, *Early Sources*. Skene, *Celtic Scotland*, Vol. II., p. 113, calls Drostan "a thoroughly Pictish name."

[3] See *Transactions of the Gaelic Society of Inverness*, Vol. XI., pp. 149-50.

[4] For St. Drostan see A. B. Scott, "St. Drostan of Buchan and Caithness" in *Transactions of the Gaelic Society of Inverness*, Vol. XXVII., pp. 110-25; also W. Mackay, "Saints Associated with the Valley of the Ness," *ibid.*, pp. 150-1—reprinted in *Sidelights on Highland History*, pp. 95-6. He must not be confused with the eighth century St. Drostan of Angus.

of the man in relation to his period and environment. St. Drostan, who was working in what is now Aberdeenshire about 520, just at the time when Columba was born, was of noble Britonic blood, and combined the advantages of high birth with great personal gifts and passionate conviction. Along with him laboured his three disciples—"Drostan and his three," they are called in the Martyrology of Oengus[1]—namely, Colm or Colman, Medan, and Fergus. The footsteps of these four evangelists in Buchan and its neighbourhood may still be traced by the associated churches which they planted. Their chief foundation was undoubtedly the monastery at Deer,[2] which after generations, confusing Colm with Columba, attributed to the great Scotic apostle. We trace St. Drostan also at Insch and Aberdour, and westward into what is now Banffshire at Rothiemay and Aberlour. St. Colm, usually disguised under the later equation with Columba, appears at Oyne, Daviot

---

[1]Ed. W. Stokes, 1905, p. 251.

[2]The site of the Celtic monastery at Deer is uncertain. Dr. John Stuart (*Book of Deer*, p. x., note 2), thought it stood at or near the old Parish Church, that is, about a mile east of the later Cistercian Abbey, and on the south or opposite side of the river Ugie. All the circumstances seem to me to point to this view being correct. The site of the Parish Church is within a bend or crook of the river, a situation again and again found at old Celtic religious centres, for example, at St. Machar's, Aberdeen ; at Dyce ; and at Machar's Haugh, Kildrummy. It is also on a knoll or mound (Tap Tillery), like the old Celtic church sites at Fetterangus, Kildrummy, Arbuthnott and St. Vigean's. An alternative site, about a mile to the south—where are still St. *Colm's* Hillock, St. *Colm's* Well, and St. Drostan's Well—is favoured by Rev. H. J. Lovibond (*The Scottish Churchman*, Vol. VI., October, 1926, p. 152). The only memorial of St. Drostan's foundation that survived almost to our own time was a cross-marked symbol-stone (Fig. 28) which used to be preserved among the monastic ruins, but has now disappeared. Its original *locus* is unknown. Almost no particulars have survived as to the history of the Celtic monastery, but the vernacular entries in the Book of Deer are evidence that it maintained its identity, and enjoyed the munificence of distinguished patrons, until as late as the twelfth century. Among those who figure as making grants to the monks of Deer are Malcolm Macmaelbrigte, Mormaeor of Moray, who died in 1029; Maelsnechtai, son of Lulach the Simpleton (stepson of Macbeth); Malcolm II. MacKenneth, King of Scotland from 1005-34; and finally, David I., whose charter, granted from Aberdeen, is in Latin. The Cistercian Abbey at Deer was founded in 1215 by William, the first Comyn Earl of Buchan, and colonised with monks from Kinloss. Whether the Celtic monastery was suppressed to make way for the Cistercians, or whether it had already decayed, we cannot tell. We are told the names of only three brethren, Hugh, Arthur and John, who were transplanted from Kinloss to Deer. The small number might afford grounds to think that these were added to some Celtic monks surviving from St. Drostan's foundation, and now, perhaps, compulsorily turned into Cistercians, as their colleagues, the Culdees at Monymusk, about the same time were transformed into Augustinians.

(with its early Pictish symbol stone[1]), Birse, Belhelvie, Monykebbock in Newmachar, and Lonmay (St. Combs), and in Banffshire at Alvah and Portsoy. It is significant that, despite the later ascription of Belhelvie to Columba, the truth survives in a rubric in the Aberdeen Breviary, which definitely states that St. *Colman* was patron of this church. St. Medan, the second of Drostan's companions, had a site at Philorth near Fraserburgh : one at Auchmedden near St. Drostan's foundation at Aberdour : one at St. Medan's Church, Cothal, Fintray ; and one at Pitmedden of Udny. St. Fergus, the third of the group, founded churches at Fetterangus (where a Pictish symbol-stone of the oldest class lies in the churchyard) ;[2] at Lungley, now the parish church of St. Fergus in Peterhead ; and at Dyce, one of the most remarkable early Christian sites in Aberdeenshire, with its splendid series of crosses and symbol-stones.[3] Drostan and his mission also worked across the water in Caithness,[4] where their church foundations occur side by side as in Buchan. Thus we have churches of St. Drostan at Canisbay,[5] Brabstermire,[6] Halkirk,[7] Olrig,[8] and Westfield ;[9] of St.

---

[1]Fig. 30.   [2]Fig. 29.

[3]The Dyce stones are illustrated at Figs. 31-3. For these Aberdeenshire sites of "Drostan and his three," see my *Origins of Christianity in Aberdeenshire*, pp. 14-16. For Portsoy, see A. Jervise, *Epitaphs and Inscriptions*, Vol. II., p. 107; and *Collections on the Shires of Aberdeen and Banff*, p. 644.

[4]According to the legend of St. Fergus, as preserved in the Aberdeen Breviary, the mission in Caithness took place prior to that in Buchan—Forbes, *Kalendars of Scottish Saints*, p. 336. There may thus be a germ of truth in the statement of the Myth of Deer that Drostan and his companions came first to Aberdour, the bay of which would be a natural place for a vessel to put into, crossing from Caithness. Presumably they would sail from Wick, where St. Fergus had a church. The map (Fig. 34) brings clearly out the significance of the associated sites of "Drostan and his three" on both sides of the Moray Firth.

[5]St. Drostan's Church, Canisbay (see *Origines Parochiales Scotiae*, Vol. II., Part II., p. 792) is one of the few medieval parochial churches remaining in Caithness, and is a structure of very great interest, dating probably in its oldest parts from the end of the fourteenth century.

[6]The site of St. Drostan's Chapel, Brabstermire, is on the west side of the turnpike near Brabstermire House. No trace of the medieval building, which was chancelled, now remains. See Rev. D. Beaton, *Ecclesiastical History of Caithness and Annals of Caithness Parishes*, p. 49.

[7]The site of St. Trostan's Chapel, with its unenclosed graveyard, is at Westerdale, about 2 miles south of Halkirk village—see O.S., 6 in., Caithness, sheet XXII. As the name (Halkirk—High Church) reminds us, it was here that the Cathedral Church of Caithness was first established, until after the brutal murder there of Bishop Adam (11th September, 1222), his successor, Bishop Gilbert de Moravia, transferred the diocesan centre to Dornoch, also an old Celtic religious site (see *supra*, p. 20).

[8]"St. Trothan's Kirk" at Olrig, now a roofless ivy-clad ruin, dates from 1633, but possesses a medieval font.

[9]"St. Trostan's Chapel" here has disappeared, but the graveyard remains, and built into its wall is an ancient font. See O.S., 6 in., Caithness, sheet XI.

Colm at Old Tain, Caithness,[1] and on the islands of Hoy and Sanday, in the Orkneys;[2] of St. Medan at Freswick[3] and possibly Bower Madan;[4] of St. Fergus at Wick[5] and perhaps at Halkirk.[6] To this northern group of sites associated with "Drostan and his three" I should be strongly inclined to add two others: the chapel-site at Eilean Coomb, in the parish of Tongue, which has been attributed to Columba; and the chapel-site and graveyard known as St. Columba's at Dirlot.[7]

Two of the later entries of grants in the Book of Deer present a feature of unmistakable significance. The first records the gift of a property "for the consecration of a church of Christ and Peter the Apostle both to Columcille and to Drostan free from all the exactions." The other is a grant of offerings "to God and to Drostan and to Columcille and to Peter the Apostle."[8] The introduction of the name of St. Peter in these grants is highly symptomatic. Not content with merging St. Colm with St. Columba, the later Romanised clergy at Deer took

[1] "St. Coomb's Kirk," on the Links of Old Tain (Parish of Olrig), is now known only by its site (O.S. Map, 6 inch, Caithness, sheet VI., and *New Statistical Account*, Vol. XV., Caithness, pp. 61-2). St. Colm or Colman also had a church at Reay, further to the west—see T. Pennant, *Tour in Scotland*, 1769 (Vth ed., 1790), Vol. I., p. 357.

[2] St. Colm's Kirk, Hoy, always so called locally. Thomas Dempster has evidently preserved a grain of the truth in his entry under 6th June (*Menologium*, ed. Bishop Forbes, *Kalendars of Scottish Saints*, p. 202)—*Kirkuae Colmi Orcadum apostoli*. *Cf.* also David Camerarius, *De Scotorum Fortitudine*, p. 113, under date 9th March, where St. Colm is styled "Bishop of the Orkneys." These entries make it quite clear that in this case the equation with Columba is entirely modern. A cross-slab found in the ruins of the old church is shown at Fig. 35. For St. Colm's of Burness in Sanday see *New Statistical Account*, Vol. XV., Orkney, p. 85.

[3] For St. Maddan's Chapel, Freswick, see *New Statistical Account*, Vol. XV., *Caithness*, p. 25.

[4] No trace of a chapel here remains, nor is one known to have existed: but the name is suggestive.

[5] Only a fragment of the old church, said to have been built by George, fourth Earl of Caithness (1529-83) now remains. It contains an effigy said to be of St. Fergus, but evidently that of a cleric of the later fifteenth century.

[6] *New Statistical Account*, Vol. XV., *Caithness*, p. 68. There are a number of unpedigreed church sites in the parish of Halkirk.

[7] North of the graveyard is a well, *Tobar Chalum Cille*, the name of which may indicate that the confusion, if there has been one, between the local St. Colm and the Abbot of Iona must have taken place at a fairly early period. Having regard to all the facts, it seems infinitely more likely that the sites at Eilean Coomb and Dirlot should be attributed to St. Colm, in or near the sphere of whose operations they lie, than to St. Columba, of whose presence in this remote northern region there is otherwise not a shred of evidence.

[8] *Book of Deer*, ed. J. Stuart, pp. 93, 95.

as their chief patron St. Peter, who in the first of these two grants is given pride of place, next to the Saviour's Name, alike over Columba and Drostan. Thus are clearly shown the stages by which the "Myth of Deer," as Macbain called it, was evolved. First Columba is made to appear as the founder of Deer, by a process of confusion with the historical St. Colm, who in actual fact was a follower of St. Drostan, the real founder of the monastery at a time when Columba was either not yet born or lying in his cradle. Secondly, to serve the purposes of the Columban legend the historical St. Drostan is taken out of his setting and made to appear as a disciple of the Abbot of Iona. And thirdly, under Roman influences in the twelfth century both St. Columba and the mythical St. Drostan are subordinated to the Apostle Peter.

How utterly impossible it would have been for Columba to plant a community at a place situated like Deer in the heart of hostile Pictland is fully apparent to all who study intelligently the political history of the times. With his love of interference in politics, and his one-sided championship of his Scotic countrymen, Columba was justly regarded with suspicion by the Pictish leaders from the High King Brude Mac-Maelchon downwards. How unfriendly his relationships were with the Pictish clergy who laboured near Iona, and with whom he was thus brought into personal contact, we know from several circumstances. In the Martyrology of Oengus, for example, an interview is preserved between St. Donnan of Eigg and St. Columba, which strikingly reveals the true relations between the Pictish Church and the intrusive Scotic Church of Iona, and also casts a somewhat lurid light upon the intolerant and prejudiced character of St. Columba. "This Donnan went to Columcille to make him his soul's friend [confessor]; upon which Columcille said to him, 'I shall not be soul's friend to a company heirs of red martyrdom: for thou shalt come to red martyrdom, thou and thy people with thee.' And it was fulfilled."[1] Readers of Adamnan's

---

[1] *Martyrology of Oengus*, ed. W. Stokes, 1905, p. 116. Yet Skene, *Celtic Scotland*, Vol. II., p. 133, includes Donnan among Columba's disciples. In point of fact there is a strong probability that he came from *Candida Casa*. This is suggested by the range of his churches, which—starting from Kirkmaiden, next door to *Candida Casa*, and extending as far as Kildonan in Sutherland—exactly follow the footsteps of St. Ninian. Moreover, many of his church sites, such as Kildonan in Colmonell, and Kildonan in Sutherland, closely adjoin foundations of St. Ninian—Scott, *Pictish Nation*, p. 268, also p. 99: see

biography will be familiar with the habit ascribed to Columba of pro-
nouncing on all who displeased him sanguinary curses that had an
awkward knack of being fulfilled.[1]   So also we have the repulsive
incident, likewise narrated by Adamnan, of Columba's savage treatment
of the penitent King Aedh Dubh of the Irish Picts, and of Abbot
Findchan, who had received the suppliant into penance.[2]   Then again
there is the curious old Hebridean account of Columba's collision with
his neighbour St. Moluag of Lismore, in which the rough blustering
character of the Scotic cleric is contrasted with the gentle nature of his
Pictish contemporary, Moluag "the pure and brilliant, the gracious and
decorous, the sun of Lismore in Alba," as his disciples loved to call
him.   The story of the encounter between the two saints, as recovered
by the Rev. D. Carmichael, Minister of Reay, a native of Lismore, is so
strikingly characteristic of the two men, and so entirely in accordance

also his paper on this Saint in *Transactions of the Scottish Ecclesiological Society*, Vol. I.,
Part III., pp. 256-67.

The martyrdom of St. Donnan took place at Eigg on Easter Day, 17th April, 618.
For the chronology see Anderson, *Early Sources*, Vol. I., p. 144.   "Red Martyrdom" was
to die for Christ: "White Martyrdom" was to suffer for Him.

[1]My critic, the Rev. C. L. Broun—whose difficulty is that unless the living figure of
St. Columba is reduced to the empty serenity of a stained glass saint, he feels himself unable
conscientiously to keep his festival—is violently annoyed with my reading of the St.
Donnan incident, of which he propounds an explanation of his own.   "Most Christians
regard 'red martyrdom' as the greatest honour that could befall any man: and there is
surely no doubt that St. Columba took that view.   It is clearer than day that the Saint, who
certainly never refused to receive a penitent of whatever nationality, regarded himself as
unworthy of the honour of being confessor to a 'noble army of martyrs.' "   Mr. Broun's
endeavour thus to explain away St. Columba's rebuff to St. Donnan is ingenious, and certainly
worth considering.   But he is not entitled to stigmatise as "a wholly perverse and cruel mis-
representation" what I submit is the natural reading of the facts, and one in harmony with
all that we know otherwise of Columba's personality.   As for the assertion that Columba
"never refused to receive a penitent," what about the case of Aedh Dubh?

Mr. Broun thus closes his letter (*Scottish Chronicle*, 5th June, 1925):—"In conclusion,
therefore, I hope that we shall keep St. Columba's Festival next week without the smallest
feeling that we have over-rated either his work or his sanctity."   But, really, we cannot
allow our judgment about a great historical personage to be determined by the necessity
of observing his day in the Calendar: nor in the case of Columba need any such difficulty
arise.   St. Ambrose and St. Augustine are names which every Christian rightly honours:
yet each of them, in actual life, must have been in some respects a decidedly
unpleasant fellow!   I must candidly confess some impatience with the stained glass theory
of Columba.   To me he is infinitely more real and attractive in all the varied tints of a
powerful and singularly complex human personality.

[2]Adamnan, Bk. I., Ch. XXXVI.

with all we know about the political situation, that it is worth reproducing in full.

"St Moluag was sailing towards Lismore when he beheld a boat carrying
St. Columba and making for the Lismore shore at highest speed.   St.
Columba's craft was the faster.   When St. Moluag saw that he was likely
to be beaten, he seized an axe, cut off his little finger, threw it on the beach,
some distance away, and cried out, 'My flesh and blood have first possession
of the island, and I bless it in the Name of the Lord.'   St. Columba, seeing
that he was outwitted, began to invoke various curses on St. Moluag's
occupation.

 ' May you have the alder for your firewood,' wished St. Columba.
 ' The Lord will make the alder burn pleasantly,' replied St. Moluag.
 ' May you have the jagged ridges for your pathways', exclaimed St.
  Columba.
 ' The Lord will smooth them to the feet,' answered St. Moluag.''

As Mr. Scott has truly remarked, "it is very interesting to find both St.
Columba and St. Moluag depicted in popular tradition exactly as they
are in these written histories which the common people never heard."[1]

Incidents such as these explain the curiously candid criticism of
the gentle Bede, who dismisses Columba with the dry remark: "of a
sooth whatever fashion of man he was himself, we are assured of this
fact at least, that he left behind him successors distinguished by great
sobriety and divine love and a strict regard for discipline." [2] Dr. Reeves,
the learned editor of Adamnan, rightly comments in his Introduction
upon "the Saint's imperious and vindictive temper," and remarks that
"with the profound respect in which his memory was held, there seems
to have been always associated a considerable degree of awe.   Hence,
perhaps, the repulsive form in which he was supposed to have presented
himself to Alexander II. in 1249."[3]   The story of King Alexander's
vision is told in an old Norse saga, which describes how as the monarch
lay asleep in the island of Kerrera, he was visited in his dreams by St.

---

[1] See *Transactions of the Scottish Ecclesiological Society*, Vol. III., Part III., p. 299.
The story is, or was, general in the Islands. The *Bachuill Mor*, or pastoral staff, of St.
Moluag is still preserved, and is shown at Fig. 36.

[2] *Verum qualiscumque fuerit ipse, nos hoc de illo certum tenemus, quia reliquit successores
magna continentia ac divino amore regularique institutione insignes*—Bede, *Ecclesiastical History*,
Bk. III., Chap. 4 (Plummer's ed., Vol. I., p. 134).

[3] Reeves, *Adamnan*, 1874, pp. xxxix-xl.

F

Olaf, St. Magnus, and St. Columba—who, we are told, "was by far the largest in figure, and the most frowning of them all."[1]

Yet, by a wonderful contrast—which only those who appreciate the Celtic character can understand—this man, so hard and bigoted in his dealings with his fellows when they differed from himself, had a strange compassion for the weak, the young, the poor, and the unfortunate, concerning which his biographer has many charming incidents to tell us. He also had a great love for the wild life of nature, and a warm-hearted sympathy with the sufferings of dumb animals. One of the most beautiful stories in Adamnan's Life describes the Saint's kindly solicitude for a poor crane that had arrived exhausted on the beach of Iona. The story is so gracefully and so tenderly told that I venture to quote it in full.[2]

"At another time, when the Saint was living in Iona, he called one of the brothers, and thus addressed him : 'In the morning of the third day from this date thou must sit down and wait on the shore on the western side of this island; for a crane, which is a stranger from the northern region of Ireland, and hath been driven about by various winds, shall come, weary and fatigued, after the ninth hour,[3] and lie down before thee on the beach quite exhausted. Treat that bird tenderly, take it to some neighbouring house, where it may be kindly received and carefully nursed and fed by thee for three days and three nights. When the crane is refreshed with the three days' rest, and is unwilling to abide any longer with us, it shall fly back with renewed strength to the pleasant part of Ireland from which it originally hath come. This bird do I consign to thee with such special care, because it cometh from our own native place.' The brother obeyed, and on the third day, after the ninth hour, he watched as he was bid for the arrival of the expected guest. As soon as the crane came and alighted on the shore, he took it up gently in its weakness, and carried it to a dwelling that was near, where in its hunger he fed it. On his return to the monastery in the evening, the Saint, without any inquiry but as stating a fact, said to him, 'God bless thee, my child, for thy kind attention to this foreign visitor, that shall not

---

[1] *Eirspennill's Hakon Hakonsson's Saga*, see Anderson, *Early Sources*, Vol. II., pp. 556-7. It is curious that the Saga describes Columba as "very bald in front," a correct description of the old Celtic tonsure which is somewhat remarkable in a Norse writer of the thirteenth century.

[2] Adamnan, Bk. I., Chap. XLVIII. The translation is that of Bishop Forbes (Reeves, *Adamnan*, 1874, pp. 34-5), with some slight changes.

[3] i.e., about three o'clock in the afternoon. The usual canonical hours, except compline, were observed by the Celtic Church.

remain long on its journey, but return within three days to its own home. As the Saint predicted, so exactly did the event prove, for after being nursed carefully for three days, the bird then gently rose on its wings to a great height, in sight of its hospitable entertainer, and marking for a little its path through the air homewards, it directed its course across the sea to Ireland, straight as it could fly, on a calm day."

Divested of the miraculous flavour with which Adamnan contrives to invest even the most ordinary anecdote about his hero's life, we have here surely a genuine and an altogether lovable tale of Columba's kindness to a forlorn, storm-beaten bird picked up on the sea shore. No re-casting of the balances can obliterate the fact that Columba was in every sense a great man : but such an incident as this proves something more, namely, that with all his patent faults of temper he was also not a bad man. If Columba appeared to King Alexander II. in rather gruesome guise, it is only right to add that in old Hebridean tradition he is grouped with Michael of the White Steed and Mary Mother as "Kind Columcille."

Throughout his years of exile in Iona Columba never lost touch with the political situation in Ireland ; and in 575, along with his recent nominee King Aidan, he paid a visit to his native land in order to attend the famous gathering at Drumceatt, a place now known as the Mullagh, or Daisy Hill in Roe Park, near Newtown Limavaddy in County Londonderry. This convention, summoned by Aedh MacAinmire, High King of Ireland, consisted of the principal chiefs and clergy throughout the country. We are told that Columba, whose self-invited return from exile was displeasing to King Aedh,[1] attended the conference for three chief reasons: first, to secure the release of Scanlann, a state prisoner in whom he was interested ; secondly, to put in a word in favour of the bards, whose status was being impugned ; and thirdly, to secure the privileges of the Dalriads, his fellow-countrymen, who still lived in Ireland. In each of these three matters Columba was completely suc-

---

[1] "So then Columba entered the assembly, and a great multitude arose before him to make him welcome. . . . But according to another old story, no one rose before him save Domnall the son of the King: for the King had said that no one should rise before him, as he, the King, knew for what Columba had come, and was not pleased at his coming, for he liked not to retain the poets or to release Scandlan." Introduction to the *Amra Choluimbchille*, ed. W. Stokes in *Revue Celtique*, Vol. XX, p. 39. *Cf* also the *Old Irish Life* in Skene, *Celtic Scotland*, Vol. II, p. 497.

cessful in gaining his own way; and it is clear from all our evidence that his powerful personality dominated the gathering. The case of Scanlann, about whose name later generations wove strange legends, need not detain us here, but the dispute about the bards and the question of the status of the Dalriads in Ireland are of more general interest.

The bards were one of the three learned orders in Celtic Ireland: the other two being the druids or magicians[1] and the brehons or judges. The bards were more than merely minstrels, they were the chroniclers and genealogists of the age, who cast events and legends and specially family trees into rhyming verse, and chanted them to musical accompaniment—with harp or pipe according to the warlike or tender nature of their theme—travelling throughout the country, and welcomed equally in cottage and palace. It is easy to understand that the less reputable among the bards would tend to degenerate into roving beggars; and, as they claimed free quarters wherever they went, they were apt to make themselves a nuisance. Their numbers increased so greatly that in Columba's time they were reckoned to be about a third of the total populace.[2] At the Convention of Drumceatt the summary abolition of the whole order was mooted, and it was this drastic proposal that drew Columba, himself a poet of no mean rank, to vigorous intervention in their favour. He pointed out the great services which the bards rendered in preserving the memory of heroic events that but for them would soon be forgotten. As a result of Columba's urgent plea the order of bards was not abolished, but their numbers and privileges were severely restricted.

Columba's intervention on behalf of his kinsmen, the Dalriads who still remained in Ireland, has been the subject of much misunderstanding. Their kingdom bore the same name, Dalriada, as that of their fellow-countrymen across the narrow waters in Argyllshire.

---

[1] To the druids belonged also the subordinate class of physicians.

[2] For the bards and their presumptions see P. W. Joyce, *Social History of Ancient Ireland*, Vol. I., pp. 455-7. The bowl which a bard carried about for receiving donations came to be known as a "cauldron of greed." Good instances of their impudence and power of intimidation are given in §§ 80-1 and 157 of O'Donnell's Irish *Life*, ed. O'Kelleher and Schoepperle, pp. 71-3, 161-5. In Scotland at a much later time the nuisance of the bards was dealt with by one of the Statutes of Iona, 1609—see the eighth Duke of Argyll, *Scotland as It was and as It is*, IInd Edition, pp. 173-4.

Owing to this fact it has been widely assumed that Columba's intervention at Drumceatt was on behalf of the Scotic colony in Pictland,
for whom it is thought that he was demanding independence from the
Ardrigh of Ireland. It has recently, however, been shown beyond doubt[1]
that it was Irish and not Pictish Dalriada whose status was in question.
Thanks to Columba's exertions the Dalriads in Ireland were freed from
paying tribute to the High King, but were held liable for military service
when required, except in the matter of ships, which were apparently to
be under the control of the King of British Dalriada.

Columba's next intrusion into Irish affairs was much less happy in
its results, and involved him, for the third time in his troubled life, in
the responsibility for an outbreak of civil war, although in this case it
is hard to say how far he was personally to blame. We have seen that
on his visit to King Brude at Inverness in 564 he had been accompanied
by the famous Iro-Pictish cleric, St. Comgall the Great of Bangor, who
in his youth had studied alongside Columba in the schools at Clonard
and Glasnevin. But it seems to have been almost impossible, under the
existing political conditions, for Pict and Scot to work long in harmony,
even under the Cross of Christ : and so about 579 Columba and Comgall
quarrelled about the jurisdiction over a church near Coleraine. As often
in Irish history, their respective clans rose in support of the rival ecclesiastical leaders, and a battle, with outcome favourable to Columba, took
place at Coleraine.

In or about the year 585 we find Columba in Ireland once again,
inspecting the monastery which he had founded at Durrow. On this
occasion also he paid a visit to the famous monastery—"*Scotorum nobile
culmen*"[2]—established by St. Ciaran at Clonmacnoise in 544 or 548.[3] In
587 a battle was fought at Cuilfetha near Clonard,[4] and in this fight
also Columba is said to have been concerned, although very little

[1]By A. O. Anderson, *Early Sources of Scottish History*, Vol. I., pp. 81-4.

[2]See Petrie, *Ecclesiastical Architecture of Ireland*, IInd ed., p. 97.

[3]For the tremendous reception which Columba was accorded there see Adamnan,
Bk. I., Chapter III.

[4]The site of this place is apparently unascertained. It was known as "the battle of the
weir of Clonard"—see Reeves, *Adamnan*, 1874, p. xlvi., and Anderson, *Early Sources*,
Vol. I., p. 98.

is known as to the nature of the quarrel, or the part which he bore in it, except that it was fought against Colman, son of Columba's old enemy, King Diarmait, and that Columba's side again came off victorious.[1]   It is recorded that in his later days remorse for the bloodshed which he had provoked in his stormy career weighed sorely upon Columba's soul, and that to ease his conscience he composed in Iona the famous Latin hymn known from its opening words as the *Altus Prosator*, of which a noble English translation was made by the late Bishop Anthony Mitchell of Aberdeen.[2]   If this splendid hymn is really from Columba's pen—and there is no reason whatever to doubt the fact—it must be accounted indeed a striking monument of the grandeur and the eloquence of his soul.   It is also an extremely self-revealing poem, which every student of Columba's character must closely study.   The late Marquis of Bute, who edited and translated the hymn, rightly calls attention to what he well describes as "a certain proclivity to dwell upon the terrible" ; and this, he remarks, "recalls that element in Columba's character which sometimes threw shadows on the brightness of his life, and infused with a certain awe the veneration which surrounded his memory after death."[3]

In the *Altus Prosator* we see Columba at his sublimest height.   The mighty, passionate, insurgent spirit of the man pours itself forth in a transcendental outburst.   But even the fiercest fire will in time grow cold: and so after all its storm and stress the great life drew to a quiet close.   If "dying to self is the secret of the Saints,"[4] then no one can deny that Columba in the last years of his earthly existence made good his title to that crowning glory.   He, like the fourteenth century mystic, had attained the life which is "fully meekened in naughting itself."   The story of Columba's last days and death, as told with much picturesque minuteness of detail by Adamnan, reaches a level of lofty and yet tender

[1] *Amra Choluimbchille*, ed. W. Stokes in *Revue Celtique*, Vol. XX., p. 435.

[2] The translation in its final form may be seen in Trenholme's *Story of Iona*, pp. 156-61; also in Canon Perry's *Anthony Mitchell, Bishop of Aberdeen and Orkney*, pp. 223-8.

[3] *The Altus of St. Columba*, ed. John, Marquis of Bute, p. iv.

[4] Lucy Menzies, *St. Margaret, Queen of Scotland*, p. 149.

beauty not often surpassed in the whole range of biographical literature, and I therefore make no apology for reproducing his account at length.[1]

'One day in the month of May the old man, worn out with age, went in a cart to visit some of the brethren who were at work. And having found them on the western side of the island, he began to speak to them, saying, 'During the Paschal solemnities in the month of April now past, with desire have I desired[2] to depart to Christ the Lord, as He had allowed me, if I preferred it. But lest a joyous festival should be turned for you into mourning, I thought it better to put off for a little longer the time of my departure from the world.' The beloved monks all the while they were hearing this sad news were greatly afflicted, and he endeavoured as well as he could to cheer them with words of consolation. Then having done this, he turned his face to the east, still seated as he was in his cart, and blessed the island with its inhabitants. . . .

"A few days afterwards, while he was celebrating the solemn offices of the Mass as usual on the Lord's Day, the face of the venerable man, as his eyes were raised to heaven, suddenly appeared as if suffused with a ruddy glow, for, as it is written, 'a glad heart maketh a cheerful countenance.'[3] For at that same hour he alone saw an Angel of the Lord hovering above within the walls of his oratory; and as the lovely and tranquil aspect of the holy Angels infuses joy and exultation into the hearts of the elect, this was the cause of that sudden joy infused into the blessed man. When those who were present on the occasion inquired as to the cause of that joy with which he was evidently inspired, the Saint looking upwards gave them this reply, 'Wonderful and unspeakable is the subtlety of the angelic nature! For lo! an Angel of the Lord, who was sent to demand a certain deposit dear to God, hath, after looking down upon us within the church, and blessing us, returned again through the roof of the church, without leaving any trace of his passage out.' Thus spoke the Saint. But none of the bystanders could understand what kind of a deposit the Angel was sent to demand. Our patron, however, gave the name of a holy deposit to his own soul that had been intrusted to him by God. . . . In the end of this same week, that is on the day of the Sabbath,[4] the venerable man and his faithful attendant, Diarmait, went to bless the barn, which was near at hand. When the Saint had entered in and blessed it, and two heaps of winnowed corn that were in it, he gave expression to his thanks in these words, saying : 'I heartily congratulate my beloved monks, that this year also, if I am obliged to depart from you, you will have a sufficient supply for the year.' On hearing this, Diarmait, his attendant,

---

[1]Adamnan, Bk. III., Ch. XXIII. The translation is that of Bishop Forbes (Reeves, *Adamnan*, 1874, pp. 94-8), with certain minor corrections.

[2]*Luke*, Ch. XXII., v. 15.

[3]*Proverbs*, Ch. XV., v. 13.

[4]Saturday, of course.

began to feel sad, and said, 'This year at this time, father, thou very often vexest us, by so frequently making mention of thy leaving us.' But the Saint replied to him, 'I have a little secret address to make to thee, and if thou wilt promise me faithfully not to reveal it to anyone before my death, I shall be able to speak to thee with more freedom about my departure.' When his attendant had on bended knees made the promise as the Saint desired, the venerable man thus resumed his address : 'This day in the Holy Scriptures is called the Sabbath, which means rest. And this day is indeed a Sabbath to me, for it is the last day of my present laborious life, and on it I rest after the fatigues of my labours; and this night at midnight, which commenceth the solemn Lord's Day, I shall, according to the sayings of Scripture, go the way of our fathers. For already my Lord Jesus Christ deigneth to invite me; and to Him, I say, in the middle of the night shall I depart at His invitation. For so it hath been revealed to me by the Lord Himself.' The attendant hearing these sad words began to weep bitterly, and the Saint endeavoured to console him as well as he could.

"After this the Saint left the barn, and in going back to the monastery rested half-way where a cross, which was afterwards erected and is standing to this day, fixed into a mill-stone,[1] may be observed on the roadside. While the Saint, as I have said, bowed down with old age, sat there to rest a little, behold there came up to him a white pack-horse, the same that used, as a willing servant, to carry the milk vessels from the cowshed to the monastery. It came up to the Saint, and, strange to say, laid its head on his bosom— inspired, I believe, by God to do so, as each animal is gifted with the know- ledge of things according to the will of the Creator; and, knowing that its master was soon about to leave it, and that it would see him no more, began to utter plaintive cries, and like a human being to shed copious tears on the Saint's bosom, foaming and greatly wailing. The attendant, seeing this, began to drive the weeping mourner away, but the Saint forbade him, saying, 'Let it alone, as it is so fond of me—let it pour out its bitter grief into my bosom. Lo! thou, though thou art a man, and hast a rational soul, canst know nothing of my departure hence, except what I myself have just told thee : but to this brute beast devoid of reason, the Creator Himself hath evidently in some way made it known that his master is going to leave it.' And saying this, the Saint blessed the work-horse, which turned away from him in sadness.[2]

[1]If the cross was fixed into a mill-stone it probably was of wood. The cross which Oswald, King of Northumbria, set up before the battle of Heavenfield in 634 was a wooden one: see Bede, *Ecclesiastical History*, Bk. III., Ch. 2 (Plummer's ed., Vol. I., p. 129).

[2]When part of an ancient entrenchment, possibly the bounding *vallum* of the early monastery, was being removed behind the house Clachanach (see Map, Fig. 2) in 1906, "the bones of a small horse were found carefully buried six feet deep in the hard stony embankment, and were restored to the earth, except a tooth. Was the horse thus honourably and laboriously interred in some past age the white horse in memory of whose farewell to his master Columba a wayside cross was set up?"—Trenholme, *Iona*, p. 102. For the horse with supernatural powers in Celtic legend see O'Donnell's *Life of Columcille*, ed. O'Kelleher and Schoepperle, pp. xvii-viii.

"Then leaving this spot, he ascended the hill that overlooketh the monastery,[1] and stood for some little time on its summit; and as he stood there with both hands uplifted, he blessed his monastery, saying:

" 'Small and mean though this place is, yet it shall be held in great and unusual honour, not only by Scotic kings and people, but also by rulers of foreign and barbarous nations and by their subjects: the Saints also even of other Churches shall regard it with no common reverence.'[2]

"After these words he descended the hill, and having returned to the monastery sat in his hut transcribing the Psalter, and coming to that verse of the 33rd Psalm,[3] where it is written, 'They that seek the Lord shall want no manner of thing that is good'—'Here,' said he, 'at the end of the page, I must stop; and what follows let Baithene write.' . . .

"Having written the aforementioned verse at the end of the page, the Saint went to church to the nocturnal vigils of the Lord's Day; and so soon as this was over, he returned to his chamber, and spent the remainder of the night on his bed, where he had a bare flag for his couch, and for his pillow a stone, which stands to this day as a kind of monument beside his grave. While then he was reclining there, he gave his last instructions to the brethren, in the hearing of his attendant alone, saying: 'These, O my children, are the last words I address to you—that ye be at peace, and have unfeigned

---

[1] "*Monticellum monasterio supereminentem ascendens.*"   If the northern site for the original monastery be accepted, this would not be the knoll *Torr Abb*, which is immediately west of the Cathedral Church, but one of the two mounds behind Clachanach, probably the one called *Cnoc-na-briste-clach*. See Skene, *Celtic Scotland*, Vol. II, p. 141, Note 29.

[2] " *Huic loco, quamlibet angusto et vili, non tantum Scotorum reges cum populis, sed etiam barbararum et exterarum gentium regnatores, cum plebibus sibi subiectis, grandem et non mediocrem conferent honorem: a Sanctis quoque etiam aliarum ecclesiarum non mediocris veneratio conferetur.*"

Like so much else that Columba did and said, his last famous prophecy also has been misunderstood, and a wider significance has been imputed to it, through a lack of appreciation of his habits of mind and of the historic conditions. The "Scotic kings and people" to whom he referred were, of course, not the later Scots of Scotland but his own kinsfolk of Dalriada and Ireland. The "rulers of foreign and barbarous nations and their subjects" would include the Picts, who were to him always a "gentile" nation that he despised. Their Church and its missionaries, with whom Columba had scanty co-operation, were counted among the "Saints even of other Churches" whom Columba would have in his mind: and in the emphatic phrase "even of other Churches" we may perhaps recognise some appreciation on Columba's part of the strongly national and partisan character that he had given to the Church of Iona—as if honour to be done to it by other branches of the Celtic Church were a thing which those who heard his prophecy would regard as something unlooked for and unexpected. Viewed in this restricted sense, Columba's dying prophecy shows a just apprehension of the nature of his own life-work: but he could not have been expected to foresee the great extension of his fame, and that of his island monastery, which would result from the rising fortunes of the Scots and their ultimate predominance in Alba. Interpreted correctly, Columba's speech seems to me to reveal most strikingly how, even to the last moment of his life, the welfare and future of the Dalriadic colony were uppermost in his heart.

[3] In our Bibles, Psalm XXXIV., v. 10.

G

charity among yourselves; and if you thus follow the example of the holy
fathers, God, the Comforter of the good, will be your Helper, and I, abiding
with Him, will intercede for you; and He will not only give you sufficient
to supply the wants of this present life, but will also bestow on you the good
and eternal rewards which are laid up for those that keep His command-
ments.' Thus far have the last words of our venerable patron, as he was
about to leave this weary pilgrimage for his heavenly country, been preserved
for recital in our brief narrative. After these words, as the happy hour of
his departure gradually approached, the Saint became silent. Then as soon
as the bell tolled at midnight,[1] he rose hastily, and went to the church; and
running more quickly than the rest, he entered it alone, and knelt down in
prayer beside the altar. At the same moment his attendant, Diarmait, who
more slowly followed him, saw from a distance that the whole interior of the
church was filled with a heavenly light in the direction of the Saint. And as
he drew near to the door, the same light he had seen, and which was also seen
by a few more of the brethren standing at a distance, quickly disappeared.
Diarmait therefore, entering the church, cried out in a mournful voice, 'Where
art thou, father?' And feeling his way in the darkness, as the brethren had
not yet brought in the lights, he found the Saint lying before the altar; and
raising him up a little, he sat down beside him, and laid his holy head on his
bosom. Meanwhile the rest of the monks ran in hastily in a body with their
lights, and beholding their dying father, burst into lamentations. And the
Saint, as we have been told by some who were present, even before his
soul departed, opened wide his eyes and looked round him from side to side,
with a countenance full of wonderful joy and gladness, no doubt seeing the
holy Angels coming to meet him. Diarmait then raised the holy right hand of
the Saint, that he might bless his assembled monks. And the venerable
father himself moved his hand at the same time, as well as he was able—
that as he could not in words, while his soul was departing, he might at least,
by the motion of his hand, be seen to bless his brethren; and, having given
them his holy benediction in this way, he immediately breathed his last. After
his soul had left the tabernacle of the body, his face still continued ruddy, and
brightened in a wonderful way by his vision of the Angels, and that to such
a degree that he had the appearance, not so much of one dead as of one alive
and sleeping. Meanwhile the whole church resounded with loud lamentations
of grief.''

So died Columba, in the very early minutes of Sunday, 9th June,
597, and in the six-and-seventieth year of his age. Three days later,
amid a wild storm of rainless wind that drew a respectful veil around
the sorrowing little community on the island, his mortal remains were
committed to the earth.

[1]For an example of a Celtic monastic bell see **Fig.** 37.

Of the long and memorable life thus brought to a close, I trust I have given, as I have sought to do, a just and an adequate picture, even if it be merely an outline. Although we cannot endow Columba with the sole credit for the evangelisation of the country we now call Scotland, we must at all events acknowledge the large share he bore in that noble work. Politically also his influence was of the utmost importance in the early history of our nation. He consolidated and revived the oppressed kingdom of the Dalriad Scots, and laid the basis of its future vigour, which ultimately was to make it the dominating partner in the four principalities that shared the soil of Alba. With the Scots rather than the Picts the future would lie, and no small share in the causes underlying this momentous fact must be assigned to the personality of Columba, who throughout the thirty-four years of his residence at Iona was a steadfast champion of the Scotic intruders and a bitter foe of the Picts. But this old racial rivalry of fourteen hundred years ago is a dim and half-forgotten story now; and we, in whose veins the blood of Pict and Scot has long since mingled, may justly hold Columba in honour as one of the greatest and, with all his faults, one of the grandest figures in the early history of our noble northern land. "Long memories make great peoples," as Montalembert wisely remarked: and it will be a sad day for Scotland when her memory becomes too short to accord due reverence to the great name of Columba.

Moreover, we must also never allow ourselves to forget that the influence of Columba, though not in his own time, was profoundly exerted in the evangelisation of England. From Iona, in the century after Columba's death, there came to the pagan Angles of Northumbria the great message of a purer faith, the White Christ joining battle with Woden and Thor. In the seventh century the two portions of Ida's realm, Bernicia north of the Tees, and Deira betwixt Tees and Humber, had drawn apart under separate lords[1]; and in 617, at the tremendous battle of the Idle River—"when the waters of the Idle ran foul with Anglian blood," men remembered centuries afterwards—Edwin of Deira slew Ethelfrid of Bernicia. Oswald, the dead king's son, a mere boy, fled north before the victor, and sought refuge in Columba's

[1]See Map, Fig. 38.

monastery at Iona, the fame of which was already noised abroad among the unconverted Teutons. Pagan and Angle though he was, the fugitive prince was received by the holy brethren with true monastic hospitality :[1] and there at Iona he grew to manhood, accepted baptism, and won the hearts of all for his noble bearing and Christian piety. Seventeen years later, in 634, the usurper Edwin having fallen in battle with the mighty warrior, Penda, King of Mercia, Oswald returned from Iona to the realm of his father. Wise in council and vigorous in arms, he was above all things a soldier of Jesus Christ, and the first act of his memorable reign was to summon missionaries from Iona to instruct his pagan subjects. And so in 635 the great and good St. Aidan,[2] fixing his bishop's stool on the Holy Isle of Lindisfarne,[3] spread the good tidings of great joy throughout the hamlets of Northumbria. "Herein," in the beautiful words of Bede, "herein did he chiefly commend his doctrine to others, in that he taught none otherwise than as he lived among his friends."[4] Like Chaucer's "povre Persoun" of seven centuries later :

> " He wayted after no pompe and reverence
> Ne maked him a spyced conscience
> But Cristes lore, and his Apostles twelve
> He taughte, but first he folwed it him-selve."

The seed planted by Oswald and Aidan blossomed and bare goodly fruit ; and the Northumbrian Church—with its marvellous artistic achievement in sculpture and illuminated work, as illustrated by the Bewcastle and Ruthwell Crosses[5] and the Lindisfarne Gospels, and with its brilliant culture, of which Bede is the choicest flower—may justly be accounted the brightest jewel in Columba's crown. Nor did the southward extension of Iona's influence pause at the frontier of

---

[1] The ruling abbot then was Fergna Brit (*circa* 607-623), the Virgnous of Adamnan, the third in succession after Columba.

[2] Oswald's request for assistance was addressed to Abbot Seghine (623-52), who sent first one Corman, after whose return, disgusted with the stubborn nature and barbarism of the Angles, Aidan was despatched to take his place.

[3] For the early stones at Lindisfarne see Appendix V., p. 60, and Figs. 39-44.

[4] *Cuius doctrinam id maxime commendabat omnibus, quod non aliter quam vivebat cum suis ipse docebat*—Bede, *Eccles. Hist.*, Bk. III., Chap V. (Plummer's ed., Vol. I., p. 135).

[5] See Appendix VI., p. 61, and Figs. 45-6.

Northumbria. In 642 the saintly King Oswald was slain in battle by
Penda of Mercia, remorseless enemy of the new faith: but his brother
Oswy carried the good work on, and in 658, at the bloody battle of the
Winwaed, the last champion of the old gods was overthrown and slain.
In gratitude for this deliverance Oswy's sister, the pious Ebba, founded
a nunnery at Coldingham, upon the bleak headland which we still know
as St. Abb's Head.[1] The very nature of the place was emblematic of
the high ideals and strenuous achievement of early Northumbrian
Christianity. As John Hill Burton finely wrote, "The storm and gloom
of precipice and ocean were in conformity with the stern purpose, the
danger, and the self-mortifying humility of the devotees."[2] Hither,
in the year 660, came the Princess Ethelreda, of the royal house of East
Anglia; and after a year's residence in the northern convent she returned
to her native fenlands to become in 673 the foundress of the stately Abbey
of Ely, which in some sort is thus a daughter of St. Ebba's monastery.
From Iona to Lindisfarne, from Lindisfarne to Coldingham, from
Coldingham to Ely—tracing thus the chain of causation, we grasp the
truth of Bishop Lightfoot's telling phrase: "Augustine was the Apostle
of Kent, but Aidan was the Apostle of England.[3]

[1]St. Ebba's convent was destroyed by the Vikings in 870, after which a gap super-
vened in the religious history of Coldingham, until in 1098 King Edgar planted a new
colony of Benedictines from Durham at the village of Coldingham, about a mile inland.
On the older site at St. Abb's Head there still remain the foundations of two churches, and
portions of the ditch and wall by which in the Celtic fashion the early religious community
was enclosed. One of these churches is evidently not of very early date, being a chancelled
building of ordinary medieval type. Alexander A. Carr in his *History of Coldingham
Priory*, published in 1836, p. 243, mentions "a small Saxon arch" as having been visible
a few years before he wrote. As the word "Saxon" was then regularly used to describe
architecture of the Norman period, it is clear that this chapel, known as St. Abb's Kirk,
must have been a subordinate cell maintained by the Benedictines. The other church on
the promontory has more primitive features, and may belong to a remoter period. It is
known as St. Ebba's Chapel.

The close connection kept up between Iona and the daughter Church of Northumbria
is shown by the fact that about 683 the monastery at Coldingham—which was a double
one, including both monks and nuns— contained a brother of Scotic race, named Adamnan—
Bede, *Ecclesiastical History*, Bk. IV., Chap. 23 (Plummer's ed. Vol. I., p. 263). No
sepulchral monuments of Celtic or Anglian character now exist at Coldingham, but on
Coldingham Hill was found a fragment of a free-standing cross-shaft, finely carved with
interlaced and zoomorphic work. It is illustrated in Fig. 47.

[2]R. W. Billings, *Baronial and Ecclesiastical Antiquities of Scotland*, Vol. I., Article
Coldingham. The letterpress of Billings' work was written by Hill Burton.

[3]*Leaders in the Northern Church*, p. 11.

Bearing all these facts in mind, no one can gainsay that the Scotic Church of Iona was emphatically one of the foremost branches of the Church Catholic, and that the fame of its forceful founder must ever bulk rightly large in the annals of missionary Christendom. For Scotland, at all events, the figure of St. Columba stands luminously forth as the most vivid, real, and commanding personality in the whole range of her early history. It is as such a living man, as a great historical character whose work can be defined and whose motives may be analysed, and not as a kind of abstract conception of missionary enterprise, that I have tried to portray Columba in the foregoing paragraphs. My definition may be faulty, and my analysis mistaken : but at all events I can take this comfort to myself, that instead of dishing up anew the usual idealised and general thesis of a saintly evangelist, I have brought my readers to grips with the ancient authorities, and have sought honestly to help them in recovering from these the true historical portrait of a great man against the background of his times.

APPENDIX I.

The Site of Columba's Monastery on Iona.

(See p. 11, note 3 and Map, Fig. 2.)

The site of the Columban monastery was about a quarter of a mile north of the present Cathedral, which—it is hardly necessary to recall—is the Benedictine Abbey founded by Reginald, Lord of the Isles, about 1200, and converted into the High Church of the Diocese of the Isles about 1507. Speaking broadly, the Cathedral Church comprises some fragments in the north of the original (thirteenth century) building, in a late Romanesque style, embodied in an almost complete reconstruction which was carried out apparently in the fifteenth century. Apart from obscure remains, the oldest building with any definite architectural characteristics among the interesting group of ruins on Iona is St. Oran's Chapel, with its late Romanesque figure-sculptured doorway, dating from the later half of the 12th century, and showing strong Irish influence in the lack of projection of the capitals. This is certainly no part of the "monastery" said to have been "rebuilt" on the island by Margaret, the Queen of Malcolm Canmore. Thus an interval of fully six hundred years intervenes between Columba's time and the oldest distinctly datable ecclesiastical buildings now extant on Iona.

The identification of the site of Columba's monastery to the north of the Cathedral was proposed by Skene (Celtic Scotland, Vol. II., pp. 95-101; see also his papers, "Notes on the Earlier Establishments at Iona," and "Notes on the History of the Ruins at Iona" in Proceedings of the Society of Antiquaries of Scotland, Vol. X., pp. 202-14, and Vol. XI., pp. 330-349), and supported by him with a large mass of evidence amounting to practical certainty. Yet Dr. Fowler (Adamnan, p. 60) says that "on the whole there is no sufficient reason to doubt that the present ruins are, as might be expected, on the original site." Probably the monastery was shifted to the southern position at the time (814-8) when it seems to have been rebuilt in stone after the Viking destructions. This would appear to be confirmed by the presence, in association with the Benedictine ruins, of remains belonging to an earlier monastery apparently of late Irish type: namely, a small church immediately north of the Cathedral choir, a larger building further to the north which may have been the refectory, the stump of a round tower west of the Cathedral, the little chamber at the north-west corner of the nave, and other traces. The small church and refectory are oriented, whereas the Benedictine Abbey is deflected widely to the south. See Trenholme, Story of Iona, pp. 118-20, and Skene, Celtic Scotland, Vol. II., pp. 297-9, 303-5, 319.

There is good reason for believing that the little chamber at the north-west corner of the Benedictine nave enclosed the shrine of Columba (see Champneys, *Irish Ecclesiastical Architecture,* p. 39). It may have been the "smaller church of Kolum-cilla," visited by Magnus Barefoot in 1098 (see Snorra Sturlasson, *Heimskringla,* c. 9)—Skene, *Celtic Scotland,* Vol. II., p. 354.

APPENDIX II.

Roman Britain and St. Ninian.

(See p. 13, note 3.)

Under the reorganisation effected by Diocletian and Constantine, the Roman Empire in the fourth century was grouped in dioceses subdivided into provinces. Over each diocese was placed a vicar, while the provinces were ruled usually by rectors. These administrative designations were afterwards taken over by the Church. The Diocese of the Britains (*Dioecesis Britanniarum Provinciarum*) comprised five provinces : but their boundaries are unknown, and the maps showing them which still appear in some of our atlases are quite unauthentic, resting upon the authority of the so-called manuscript of "Richard of Cirencester," a spurious composition of an eighteenth century forger. It is necessary to emphasise this fact, because the prevalence of Richard of Cirencester's map has given rise to the belief, by no means wholly yet eradicated, that the province of Valentia, added to the diocese by Theodosius after his successful campaign against the Picts, Scots, and Saxons in 368-9, comprised the country between the two Roman Walls ; and, therefore, that in St. Ninian's time the Roman frontier extended between the Forth and the Clyde. But archæological research has made it absolutely certain that the Antonine Wall, and the country between it and Hadrian's Wall, had been lost to Rome before the end of the second century. Only certain forts, such as High Rochester (*Bremenium*), Risingham (*Habitancum*), Netherby (*Castra Exploratorum*), Bewcastle, and possibly Cramond, were held as advanced posts to Hadrian's Wall until well into the third century. Also there is some very slight and doubtful evidence for a temporary re-occupation of the station at Birrens (*Blatobulgium*) in the reign of Constantine (but see Sir George Macdonald in *Proc. Soc. Ant. Scot.,* Vol. LII., p. 218-9). But there is no foundation whatsoever for the idea that Valentia was the recovered territory between the walls. It rests solely upon the apocryphal authority of Richard, and is completely negatived by the entire result of archæological research upon Roman sites in Scotland. With the exception of the scanty traces of later occupation noted above, these sites when excavated yield each and all a unanimous story of abandonment or destruction about the year 181. The true position of the Roman frontier must be understood in order to obtain a correct historical setting for Ninian's missionary effort. For example, much of the able work of the Rev. A. B. Scott (see his *St. Ninian, the Apostle of the Britons and the Picts,* and his *The Pictish Nation, its People and its Church*) is vitiated by the assumption that in Ninian's time the Roman frontier was the Antonine Wall.

The actual position on the frontier at Ninian's time is extremely obscure. Coin finds strongly suggest that Hadrian's Wall had been abandoned at the date of the insurrection of Magnus Maximus in 383, although some of its supporting depots like Carlisle (*Luguvallium*) Corbridge (*Corstopitum*) and the port of South Shields were held undoubtedly as late as 395. The whole position has been fully reviewed in *Journal of Roman Studies,* vol. XII., by Mr. R. G. Collingwood, who points out (p. 76) that "no single wall fort has ever produced a coin datable to a later year than 383, and that where exploration has been reasonably complete the coins always come down to within a few years of that date." The earliest Christian tombstones at Whithorn and Kirkmadrine, dating from St. Ninian's time or very shortly thereafter, clearly commemorate members of a Romanised congregation. They are written in the debased Latin language and script of the Lower Empire, they exhibit the "Chi-Rho" symbol, the Alpha and Omega, and the *Hic iacit* formula found on Imperial Roman Christian tombs, and they commemorate persons with Latin or Latinised Celtic names (see Figs. 48-9, 66-7). This is entirely in accordance with a mass of other evidence that in the fourth and fifth centuries the inhabitants of the country south of the Forth, although politically outwith the boundary of the Empire, were largely Romanised through centuries of commercial intercourse. See on this question Dr. R. Munro, *Ancient Scottish Lake Dwellings,* p. 277, and reports by A. O. Curle and J. E. Cree on the excavations at Traprain Law in *Proc. Soc. Ant. Scot.,* specially Vol. L., pp. 139-42, Vol. LIV., pp. 99-100, and Vol. LVIII., p. 282; also *Royal Commission on Ancient Monuments, Report on East Lothian,* pp. 94-9.

A true understanding of Ninian's position in relation to the Roman Empire also suggests another consideration. It has been usual to picture him as a monastic leader after the pattern which the Celtic Church developed in Ireland during the fifth and sixth centuries; and of course it is certain that Ninian was profoundly influenced by St. Martin of Tours, the founder of Celtic missionary monasticism, and that his monastery of *Candida Casa* was a great centre of evangelic activity in Pictland. Yet bearing in mind the fact that Ninian was a Romanised Briton and a subject of the Empire, and that his congregation at *Candida Casa* were certainly Romanised and Latin speaking (as their tombstones show to this day) it is also possible that the Ninianic Church in Galloway may have been organised more after the pattern of the territorial episcopal dioceses in the contemporary Roman Empire. This view appears to have been held by Skene (*Chronicles of the Picts and Scots,* Preface, p. clii.). If true, it would help to explain the subsequent organisation of the Britonic Kingdom of Strathclyde. In this connection Mr. A. O. Anderson writes me suggestively as follows. "It would appear reasonable to assume

H

that Ninian, under Roman protection, went to the districts that were more directly under Roman dominion ; and conversely, that those districts to which he can be shown to have gone were more directly under the Romans. Further, there can be little doubt that the effect of Ninian's mission was to assist the formation of the post-Roman Kingdom of Northern Britain. Hence there might be a kind of presumption that Ninian's bishopric was of similar extent to that of the North-British Kingdom. . . . Kentigern, no doubt, claimed the same territory for his bishopric, the British Church regarding civil and ecclesiastical dominion as having the same extent."

APPENDIX III.

Scoto-Pictish Relationships.

(See p. 21, note 1.)

Mr. John Gavin Tait, writing in *Aberdeen Press and Journal,* 1st February, 1926, attempts to refute my view of Scoto-Pictish relationships, pointing out that "there is no record of hostilities between Picts and Scots before 560. Previously they had been allies against the Romans and Britons." But surely Brude MacMaelchon's campaign in 560 speaks for itself. If the presence of the Scots in Pictland was not resented, then Brude's treatment of them was an odd way of showing it. I do not profess to understand the difference which Mr. Tait draws between "Romans" and "Britons" at the period with which we are concerned : but while in the fourth century Scots and Picts may have combined in raiding the Roman diocese, it was a different matter now when the Scots had taken to settling in Pictland on their own account. And on a point of detail I should like to remark that it is not certain whether the Scots and Picts were allies against the Roman diocese : Ammianus and other writers merely say that their raids synchronised. That they should have combined is *a priori* likely enough, but it is not proven. One must always remember that the word "Scot," as used by the late Roman writers, is equivalent to an inhabitant of Ireland, and so the Scotic raiders in the fourth century may have come from districts quite out of touch with the Picts. *Cf.* Claudian, *Panegyricus de Quarto Consulatu Honorii,* 33 : *"Scottorum tumulos flevit glacialis Hiverne,"* and *De Consulatu Stilichonis,* II. 251-2 : *"totam cum Scottus Ivernen movit."* After the Scotic settlement in Argyll the hostile relations between Scots and Picts are amply vouched for from the days of Brude MacMaelchon, through those of Adamnan (679-704), who speaks of the Picts as "gentiles" and "barbarians," to the period of Angus I. MacFergus (729-61) the powerful Pictish King who for the time being reduced Dalriada, storming its capital Dunadd. It does not seem to weigh against all this evidence that— as Mr. Tait points out in a further letter (see *Aberdeen Press and Journal,* 5th February, 1926)—the Pictish King Brude MacBile (672-93) is said to have been lamented by Adamnan and to have been buried at Iona. Even if the story —which occurs in an Irish life of Adamnan (Skene, *Chronicles of the Picts and Scots,* pp. 408-9)—be accepted as true in substance (and its complexion is wildly miraculous), it may be explained by the fact that there is some evidence of a temporary *rapprochement* between Picts and Scots in their common dread of the expansive policy of Ecgfrith, King of the Angles, whom Brude MacBile destroyed in the famous battle of Dunnichen (685). One can readily perceive how the Pictish King, facing the Anglian menace, would desire to secure his flank by an understanding with the Scots.

APPENDIX IV.

Brude MacMaelchon's Overlordship of Dalriada.

(See p. 21, note 3.)

The sudden check given to the pretensions of the Scots by Gabhran MacDomongart's disaster in 562 is revealed in the language of Tigernach, who speaks of Gabhran and his two predecessors as *Ri Alban,* but Conall and those who follow him are merely *Ri Dalriada*—Tigernach, *Annals,* ed. W. Stokes in *Revue Celtique,* Vol. XVII., pp. 125, 136, 142, 151, 179, 180. The title of *toshach* is applied to King Conall in the *Annals of the Four Masters* (ed. J. O'Donovan, vol. I., p. 204). This is a seventeenth century compilation (1632-6) :   and Mr. Tait, accordingly, rejects its attribution of the title *toshach* to Conall MacComgall (see his letter in *Aberdeen Press and Journal,* 1st February, 1926).   But, however this may be, the entries in Tigernach (died 1088) an authority of high importance, seem to be quite unmistakable. That the change in status of the Dalriadic rulers after Gabhran was due to their acceptance of Pictish overlordship, subsequent to Brude's victory, is confirmed, I think, by two parallel pieces of evidence :   St. Berchan's remark, quoted in the text, about "an Irishman ruling in the east under the Picts," and the probability, discussed *supra,* p. 11, note 1, that although the grant of Iona to Columba was made in the first place by the ruler of Dalriada, it required confirmation by King Brude. Mr. Tait, in his subsequent letter (5th February, 1926), challenging my statement that the title King of Alba, arrogated by the earlier Scotic rulers, was changed to King of Dalriada in consequence of the recognition of Pictish overlordship, proceeds to comment :   "but if Conall continued to be called a King, how did he 'forgo his royal status?' " Surely this is merely playing with words. After the Treaty of Falaise in 1174, William the Lion continued to bear the title King of Scots, yet in accepting Henry's overlordship had he not forgone his royal status?

APPENDIX V.

THE EARLY STONES AT LINDISFARNE.

(See p. 52, note 3.)

The early Christian stones remaining at Lindisfarne have recently been exhaustively studied by Mr. C. R. Peers, H.M. Chief Inspector of Ancient Monuments, who has clearly brought out their connection with the Celtic Church. See his paper on "The Inscribed and Sculptured Stones of Lindisfarne" in *Archæologia,* 1923-4 (Vol. LXXIV.), pp. 255-70. Mr. Peers shows that the oldest group of grave-stones at Lindisfarne (see Figs. 39, 40) are small rectangular slabs with round heads and crosses either of Latin or of Celtic type, in the latter case sometimes showing interlaced ornament. They mostly bear bi-literal inscriptions commemorating a single person, whose name is written in runes and in Hiberno-Saxon capitals. In addition to the group of a dozen from Lindisfarne, a number of similar stones, of which seven have survived (see Fig. 41), were found in 1833 at Hartlepool, a monastery founded under St. Aidan's influence in 640. "These grave-stones," observes Mr. Peers, "dating as they must from the early days of Christianity in Northumbria, have hitherto been found only at two monastic sites, both directly connected with Iona." No similar monuments have been discovered at Iona itself; but, as Mr. Peers pertinently reminds us, "it must be remembered that no systematic excavation of the early site at Iona has yet been attempted." In any case, the remoter *provenance* of this type of monument is not in doubt, for Mr. Peers clearly shows that "if anything like a close parallel is to be found, it is to Ireland we must go." He points out that a group of extremely similar stones occurs at Clonmacnoise (see Fig. 42, and *cf.* Champneys, *Irish Ecclesiastical Architecture,* p. 76). "The Irish stones," remarks Mr. Peers, "are of irregular shape, and generally much larger; and where, in a few cases, it is possible to date them with some confidence, the dates fall within the ninth and tenth centuries. That some of the stones are older than this is quite probable; and as Clonmacnoise was founded in 547, a seventh or eighth century date may reasonably be assumed in certain cases, and the more so since no other form of early grave-stone is found there." Apart from the Clonmacnoise group, this type of grave-stone is elsewhere extremely common in Ireland, but it nowhere occurs in Northumbria except at the two sites, Lindisfarne and Hartlepool, both directly connected with Aidan and the mission from Iona.

The later crosses at Lindisfarne show the blending of Roman with Celtic influences, and the modification of both by the native Anglian art, just as one would expect from the history of Northumbrian Christianity. Also as one would expect in an art taking origin from an external impulse, the earlier stones are the best, and a progressive degeneration can be traced until the rough stones wrought during the period of decay and Viking invasion in the ninth century. The monastery on Holy Isle was abandoned in 875, and the site thereafter lay derelict until the founding of the Benedictine Priory at the end of the eleventh century. Mr. Peers divides the later stones of the original monastery into three groups :—(1) Those showing good work of Irish type (Fig. 43) ; (2) those showing interlacings of good style, with animal and figure subjects, and traces of Irish motives; and (3) rougher work, with interlacings, animals, and figure subjects. With one exception—a recumbent cross slab (Fig. 43)—all the stones are fragments of free standing crosses of Irish type. In a category by itself is a standing slab with rounded head (Fig. 44), having on one side a Celtic cross with sun, moon and adoring angels, and on the other a procession of military figures. The whole character of this monument recalls the Pictish sculptured stones, and its presence among the Lindisfarne group is most remarkable. Otherwise the art relations of the Lindisfarne stones are just what we should expect them to be ; and these monuments form an altogether significant and deeply interesting archæological commentary upon the extension of the Irish Church through Iona into Northumbria.

APPENDIX VI.

The Ruthwell and Bewcastle Crosses.

(See p. 52, note 5.)

An analytical study of the art relationships discernible in these two splendid monuments (Figs. 45-6) shows clearly how they form a most instructive archæological commentary upon the composite sources of the Northumbrian Christianity that gave them origin. The Scotic or Irish archetypal element in that Christianity is revealed in the panels of inter-laced pattern on the Bewcastle Cross, a form of ornament that the Anglian sculptors borrowed from Celtic art, and also in the Roman lettering on both crosses, which is neither Latin nor Gaulish in type, but belongs to the distinctive Hiberno-Saxon school. For the Anglian element, or racial foundation, speak the form of the Ruthwell cross-head, the Anglian runes on both crosses, and particularly the famous poem inscribed in runes on the Ruthwell Cross, in which with a thoroughly Teutonic and, indeed, largely pagan spirit the Cross itself describes its part and emotions in the greatest of sagas, the tragedy of Our Lord's Passion :—

> " Then the Young Hero, who was mightiest God
>   Strong and with steadfast mind
> Up to the Cross with steps unfaltering trod
>   There to redeem mankind.
> I trembled, but I durst not fail :
> I on my shoulders bare the Glorious King.
> They pierce my sides with many a darksome nail,
> And on us both their cruel curses fling."

Anglian feeling also appears in the skill with which animal, and especially bird life, is portrayed on the two monuments. And lastly, the Roman Church influence, that was making itself felt with emphasis in Northumbria after the Synod of Whitby in 664, comes out strongly in the vine-leaf ornament and in the beautiful sculptured figures, which are entirely classical in inspiration. Indeed, the feeling of this figure sculpture on both crosses is Byzantine or Hellenistic rather than Romanesque, and reminds us that, at the time when the two crosses were in all probability set up, the dominating figure in the English Church was Theodore of Tarsus. No two monuments could together supply a more complete and interesting key to the culture of which they are the product.

Notes on Churches ascribed to St. Columba.

It is symptomatic of the way in which writers upon St. Columba have been content with generalities, instead of endeavouring to ascertain the real scope and nature of his work, that since Dr. Reeves in 1857 published his list of churches and other sites in Scotland, bearing or reputed to bear Columba's name, no systematic effort has been made to submit them to analysis—to distinguish those churches which may be genuine foundations from those that are probably medieval dedications, and those whose association with the great name of Columba seems to have resulted from confusion with some local saint like Colm of Caithness and Buchan, or Colmoc of Angus.[1]

In the case of Columba, the problem presents difficulties of unusual magnitude: some of which, in default of evidence, are perhaps now incapable of solution. A church bearing Columba's name may be one of four things. It may be (1) an original foundation by the saint in person; or (2) a church planted afterwards from Iona, and taking the name of the mother-house's founder; or (3) a medieval dedication; or (4) a medieval or modern obliteration of a local saint bearing a name similar to Columba's. Most of the churches in the Western Highlands and Islands, bearing the name Kilcolumcille, probably belong to classes (1) and (2); though how many of them may actually have been founded by Columba it is now impossible to tell. In the *Landnamabok* there is an interesting record of a Norseman, Orlyg the Old, who, *circa* 874-900, migrated from the Hebrides to Iceland, and there built a church, which he "hallowed to Columcille." The same chronicle also records the dedication by Halldor the Red of another Icelandic church to Columcille.[2] What occurred in Iceland doubtless also took place often in Scotland. With one or two exceptions, to which attention is called below, I should be highly suspicious of all churches ascribed to Columba within the limits of ancient Pictland. At all events a large proportion of them can distinctly be shown to belong to classes (3) or (4). Still less can we admit Columban foundations within the Anglian kingdom of Bernicia, which remained pagan until half a century after Columba's death, and with which there is no evidence that he had any dealings. The few churches in Strathclyde must also be

[1] Precisely the same phenomenon has taken place in Ireland. Thus at the monastery of Inis Cealtra the local hermit, Colum, was equated with the great St. Columcille. See Dr. R. A. S. Macalister in *Proc. Royal Irish Academy*, Vol. XXXIII., Section C (1916), p. 128.

[2] See A. O. Anderson's *Early Sources of Scottish History*, Vol. I., p. 343, note 1.

regarded as suspect : in Columba's time the Britonic kingdom had its own Church, with very active and distinguished missionaries, and none of the sites suggested for Columba within the kingdom of Strathclyde affords any evidence of dating back to the Celtic period.

The list and analysis submitted herewith make no pretence to be exhaustive or final.   They are offered merely as a tentative or provisional effort towards making good a deficiency, fully to resolve which requires a greater amount of research, and a wider acquaintance with the topography of Scotland, than I can claim to have employed or to command.   I shall be very grateful to receive criticisms, suggestions, and further information from any of my readers.

Unless otherwise specified, the authorities for the sites, and detailed particulars, will be found in Reeves, *Adamnan*, 1857, pp. 289-98 and 462.

I.—Church Sites within the Sphere of Columba's Influence, West of Drumalban.

1. SOROBY, Tiree.   See p. 19, note 4.

2. KIRKAPOL, Gott Bay, Tiree. A letter is addressed by Pope Gregory XI. to the Bishop of Lismore, 20th September, 1375, in favour of " *Ayg' Mac Petri perpetui vicarij parrochialis ecclesie sancte Columbe de Kerepol Sodorensis diocesis.*"   Here are " three separate sites close together ; a very old chapel upon a rock and unenclosed ; another medieval church within its graveyard ; and (nearest the shore) a burial ground without any existing remains of a former chapel."   In the medieval chapel and graveyard are some fourteen grave-slabs of late West Highland type, one inscribed with the name of *Fingonius Prior de Y* and the date 1495.   The burial ground near the shore bears the name *Cladh Odhrain* (St. Oran's graveyard), and contains two West Highland slabs and part of a free-standing cross. Remains of a fine cross formerly here, and now at Inverary Castle, are illustrated by Stuart, *Sculptured Stones of Scotland*, Vol. II., plate lii.   See Erskine Beveridge, *Coll and Tiree*, pp. 147-50, with illustrations ; also D. MacGibbon and T. Ross, *Ecclesiastical Architecture of Scotland*, Vol. I., pp. 87-9 ; and J. Anderson, *Scotland in Early Christian Times*, First Series, p. 67.

3. ELACHNAVE. Probably the *Hinba* of Adamnan : but *cf.* Watson, *Celtic Place Names of Scotland*, pp. 81-4.   See p. 22, note 2.   This island, with its most interesting group of Celtic monastic remains, is intimately associated in local tradition with Columba.   A spring on the shore is known as *Tobar Challum-na-chille*. See Reeves, *Adamnan*, 1874, pp. 318-24,

and Champneys, *Irish Ecclesiastical Architecture*, pp. 20-2, who points out that the present dry-stone buildings, primitive though they are, "probably represent a very early rebuilding in stone of a still earlier wooden monastery." An upright slab with incised cross in the burial ground is shown at Fig. 50.

4. LOCH COLUMKILLE, Skye. See p. 28, note 2.

5. FLADDA CHUAIN, or FLADDA HUNA, a small island lying to the north-west of the extreme point of Skye. Here was a chapel dedicated to St. Columba, and a burial place called *Cladh Mhanaich*, "Monks' graveyard."

6. EILEAN TRODDAY, a small island to the north-east of the foregoing, close in to the Aird of Skye. It possessed a chapel dedicated to St. Columba.

7. SKEABOST, "*Sanct Colmez Kirk*," see p. 28, note 2. This site is associated with a Pictish symbol-stone (Fig. 18), and is in all probability not to be assigned to Columba. On an islet in the river Snizort here are ecclesiastical remains of much interest, consisting of a group of six chapels enclosed by a rampart. Two of them are in fair preservation, and are good examples of the primitive featureless Hebridean church. A baptismal font remains. "On making the shore one is immediately struck with the intensely ecclesiastical character of the spot. From end to end the islet is covered with the remains of chapels." See T. S. Muir, *Ecclesiological Notes on Some of the Islands of Scotland*, p. 272.

8. EILEAN COLUIMCILLE, an island in Portree Bay, with remains of a church and graves. The inner part of the bay was formerly called *Loch Coluimcille*. See Reeves, *Adamnan*, 1874, p. 275.

9. GARIEN, in the parish of Stornoway, on the north shore of Broad Bay, on the north-east side of Lewis. Here was St. Colm's Church. Its connection with Columba is very doubtful.

10. EYE peninsula, Lewis. On this almost detached piece of land, which juts out into the Minch, east of Stornoway, stood a church called St. Collum's in Ui, an old burial place of Clan Macleod. There seems to be no evidence to connect it with Columba. The ruins now extant are of different dates, the eastern part primitive, the western perhaps Norman. See W. C. Mackenzie, *The Book of the Lews*, pp. 137-8, and illustration opp. p. 144; also MacGibbon and Ross, *Ecclesiastical Architecture of Scotland*, Vol. I., pp. 91-2.

11. EILEAN CHALUIMCHILLE, in Loch Erisort, on the east side of Lewis, south of Stornoway. On the island are a ruined church and

I

graveyard, and the inlet on the north is known as Loch Colmkill.   The existing church ruin seems to be of medieval date.   See MacGibbon and Ross, *Ecclesiastical Architecture*, Vol. I., pp. 97-8.

12. BERNERAY, an island in the Sound of Harris, close to North Uist, had a chapel named after St. Columba.

13. KILCHALMKIL, in the parish of Sand, on the north coast of North Uist.   "Indistinct traces of the south wall" still remain, on the west side of an uninclosed burial ground.   Half a mile to the south is *Tobar Chaluim Chille*.   The sites of what seems to have been the sanctuary crosses—one named *Crois Aona'ain*, Adamnan's Cross—are still known; and traces of kitchen middens may possibly represent the rubbish heaps of the community which the chapel served.   See Erskine Beveridge, *North Uist*, pp. 276-8: the chapel-site is illustrated opposite p. 276.

14. BENBECULA.   A church at Balivanich, on the north side of the island, was called *Kilcholambkille*, or *Teampull Chalumchille*.   In a charter of James V, 1535, it is described as "*ecclesia parochialis Sancti Columbe in Beandmoyll*"—*Registrum Secreti Sigilli Regum Scotorum*, Vol. II., No. 1881. For the ruins of the church see MacGibbon and Ross, *Ecclesiastical Architecture*, Vol. I., pp. 88-9.   The nave is of primitive type, with a chancel added apparently in the fourteenth century.   The word *teampull* suggests a late foundation—see *supra*, p. 19, note 4.

15. HOWMORE, at the north-west corner of South Uist.   Here is *Teampull Cholumcille*.   See Erskine Beveridge, *South Uist*, Map.   There was here a group of five chapels, one of medieval type and the others apparently of earlier date.   See T. S. Muir, *Ecclesiological Notes*, pp. 50-1, 280; also MacGibbon and Ross, *op. cit.*, Vol. I., pp. 70-1.

16. ST. KILDA.   On this remote island were three chapels, dedicated to Christ, St. Columba, and St. Brendan.   Not a vestige of these churches now remains, though the sites are known.   The festival of St. Columba was observed on the island.   A cross-marked stone is, or was, extant in the wall of a house.   The origin of the name St. Kilda is uncertain, no saint of this name being otherwise known: for a suggested explanation, see Watson, *Celtic Place Names of Scotland*, p. 98.   On the island is St. Kilder's Well—*Origines Parochiales Scotiae*, Vol. II., p. 380.   The native name for the island is Hirta.

17. CANNA.   The church on this island bore the name of St. Columba. The ruined church stands in a glen in the middle of the island, surrounded by the graveyard, in which is a fine though much damaged free-standing

cross (Fig. 51). Another fragment of an enriched cross-shaft was found near by (Fig. 52).

18. ISLAND COLUMBKILL, in Loch Archaig, parish of Kilmallie, Inverness-shire (about 10 miles north of Fort William). On the island is a ruined chapel, with the burial place of the Camerons of Lochiel—see *Ordnance Gazetteer of Scotland*, Vol. I., p. 61.

19. KILCHALLUMKILL, a chapel at Duror, in Appin, on the peninsula between Loch Creran and Loch Linnhe.

20. KILCOLMKILL, now Kiel in Ardchattan.

21. KILCOLMKILL, a ruined chapel at Kiel on Loch Aline, in the parish of Morven, Argyllshire. Beside the chapel stands a noble foliaceous cross of late West Highland type, illustrated by Stuart, *Sculptured Stones of Scotland*, Vol. II., plate xlix.

22. KILCOLLUMKILL, Quinish, at the north end of Mull.

23, SALEN, Mull. The village was formerly called *Salen-dubh-Challum-chille*, and near it were the remains of a cell.

24. ORONSAY. See p. 9, note 2.

25. CILL CHALLUIM CHILLE, or Keills, 1½ miles south-west of Port Askaig, in Kilarrow Parish, Islay. "Very little of the building is left, nor is there any remnant of dressed stone on window or door. In the crowded and ill-kept churchyard there is only one carved stone to be seen"—a late West Highland slab, with sword, galley, casket, and foliaceous ornament. See R. C. Graham, *The Carved Stones of Islay*, p. 26, and plate i.

26. KILCHOLMKILL, or CALLUMKILL, in the parish of Kildalton, Islay. "A church site, and near it a well into which offerings were at one time dropped."—Graham, *op. cit.*, p. 81. In a presentation of 1502, it is referred to as the "chapellanry of Sanct *Colme*": but in a similar writ of 1542 it appears as *capella Sancti Columbi*. See *Registrum Secreti Sigilli Regum Scotorum*, Vol. I., No. 911; Vol. II., No. 4566.

27. COVE, in South Knapdale, on the west side of Loch Caolisport, and near its head. Here there is a chapel named after St. Columba, and near it a cave with a rudely built altar, and a piscina and small cross, both cut in the rock. See *New Statistical Account*, Vol. VII., p. 263, also Capt. T. P. White, *Archæological Sketches in Scotland, Knapdale and Gigha*, pp. 56-7, and plate xiii. Dr. Skene, *Celtic Scotland*, Vol. II., p. 86, suggested that this cave, "which tradition says was Columba's first church in Scotland before he sailed to Iona, is probably connected with his residence with King Conall" (see *Adamnan*, Bk. I., ch. viii).

28. KILCOLUMKILL, at Kiels, between Carskay and Dunaverty, in Kintyre. "St. Collomkill's Church" here is mentioned in 1326. The church shows a primitive chancel with a nave apparently of Norman work —see MacGibbon and Ross, *Ecclesiastical Architecture*, Vol. I., p. 92.

29. ARRAN. In this island the following sites associated with Columba have been noted:—(1) *Tobar Chalumchille*, Columba's Well, on the north-west coast; (2) *Columbcille*, at the south end; and (3) *Suidhe Challum Chille*, Columba's chair, in Glen Suidhe. The authenticity of the last of these is doubtful. See W. M. Mackenzie in the *Book of Arran*, Vol. II., p. 68, note 1. "The Columba names in Arran," writes Mr. Mackenzie, "are few and not particularly significant: they suggest nothing for the sixth century, though it is barely credible that Christianity had not reached this outlier of the Dalriadic kingdom, which was Christian long before Columba came in 563."

30. ST. COLUMBA'S CHAPEL, BUTE. There is extant a deed of presentation in the name of James V., 26th May, 1516, to the "*capelle sive capellanie S. Calumbei infra Insulam de Bute situate*"—*Registrum Secreti Sigilli*, Vol. I., No. 2775. The site of this chapel is unknown. See the Rev. J. King Hewison, *The Island of Bute in the Olden Time*, Vol. I., p. 157. I suspect that this chapel may be the same as the chapel of St. Colmoc, or Calmag (*Kilmachalmaig*), in North Bute, between Etterick Bay and Kames Bay, where there still remains a pillar stone with wheeled and shafted cross cut out in relief. See *op. cit.*, Vol. I., pp. 116-7; also Stuart, *Sculptured Stones*, Vol. II., plate lvi. Close to the chapel site is a fine stone circle.

II.—Church Sites East of Drumalban, which have been ascribed to St. Columba, but in most cases can be shown to be unconnected with him.

The following twelve sites seem to be foundations of St. Colm of Caithness and Buchan (see pp. 36-8).

31. ST. COLM'S, Burness, Sanday, Orkneys.

32. ST. COLM'S, Hoy, Orkneys. An incised cross found here is shown at Fig. 35.

33. ST. COOMB'S, Olrig, Caithness.

34. "ST. COLUMBA'S," Dirlot, Caithness.

35. EILEAN COOMB, Tongue, Sutherland.

36. St. Colm's, Alvah, Banff.

37. St. Colm's, Portsoy, Banff.

38. St. Combs, Lonmay, Aberdeenshire.

39. St. Colm's, Daviot, Aberdeenshire. Here there is an early Pictish symbol stone (Fig. 30).

40. St. Colm's, Belhelvie, Aberdeenshire.

41. St. Colm's, Monykebbock, Aberdeenshire.

42. St. Colm's, Birse, Aberdeenshire.

43. Kilcolmkill, in Strathbrora, Sutherland, has been shown by the Rev. A. B. Scott, *Pictish Nation*, p. 384, to be a corruption of the personal name *Gillecallomgill* (A.D. 1456), which means " servant of Columcille."

44. Petty, Nairnshire, see p. 27, note 2. In all probability this is a dedication of the medieval period. In a recent work, *The Lordship of Petty*, by the late Mr. George Bain, pp. 9-10, will be found a good example of the loose and imaginative writing that has helped so largely to obscure the historical St. Columba.

45. Auldearn, Nairnshire. The patron saint is given as Columba, but St. Colm's Fair was held here. See Geo. Bain, *Hist. Nairnshire*, Vol. I., p. 37.

46. Kingussie, Inverness-shire, see p. 29.

47. Invermoriston, Loch Ness, see p. 29. These two churches may be genuine Columban foundations.

48. Cortachy, Forfarshire. Here St. Colm's Fair was held.

49. Tannadyce, Forfarshire. Here there was a chapel, apparently of unknown dedication, and not far from it, St. Colm's Well. The parish church is named after St. Ternan. In the churchyard wall, towards the end of the eighteenth century, was found an early sculptured stone, long since lost. From the description in the old *Statistical Account* (1797), Vol. IX., p. 376, it must have been an interesting example of the elaborately sculptured Forfarshire slabs. " It exhibits the figure of a man, very rudely cut, with his head uncovered, and having a loose garment, like a Highland plaid, thrown over his shoulders. With the one hand he lays hold of the mouth of an animal, which has been thought to be a lion, but has more the appearance of a wild boar. With the other, he brandishes a sword or dagger, with which he threatens destruction to his prey. There has been an inscription over the head of this figure, as would seem, in Saxon

characters. But only two or three of these are now discernible; as the stone has not only been broken into two pieces, but has been otherwise mutilated, by the unsparing hands of some workmen employed to repair the wall."

50. KIRRIEMUIR, Forfarshire. See Bishop A. P. Forbes, *Kalendars of Scottish Saints*, p. 307. But the chapel here is referred to as *capella sancti Colmoci*—see *ibid.*, p. 305. The site of the chapel is at Muirhouse—A. Jervise, *Epitaphs and Inscriptions*, Vol. II., p. 357. Probably to the same St. Colmoc should be ascribed the previous two neighbouring sites. Kirriemuir was evidently an important centre of Pictish Christianity, as appears from the five splendid sculptured slabs (Figs. 53-4), which have been discovered in the old churchyard.

51. DUNKELD. It is distinctly stated in the *Pictish Chronicle* that the church of Dunkeld was founded by Constantine I. MacFergus, King of the Picts, who reigned from 789-820—Skene, *Chronicles of the Picts and Scots*, pp. 201-2. There is not a shred of evidence of any kind that a previous church existed here. Doubtless the church was dedicated to St. Columba after Kenneth MacAlpin removed his relics thither in 849 (see p. 31). Mr. Anderson (*Early Sources*, Vol. I., p. 279, footnote 4) suggests, with great probability, that the church built by Constantine may have been destroyed by the Danes, who " wasted Dunkeld " in Kenneth's reign (Skene, *op. cit.*, p. 8). Apparently the remnants of the older Pictish community survived as a college of Culdees. The ecclesiastical antiquity of Dunkeld is vouched for by the existence here of no less than five early Celtic sculptured slabs (see Figs. 55-6). In the King's Park is St. Colme's Well.

52. ARNGASK, Perthshire. A chaplainry of St. Columba was founded here by Sir Andrew Murray of Balvaird, 1st October, 1527. See the deed of foundation in the *Registrum de Cambuskenneth*, ed. W. Fraser, pp. 34-8. The chapel was founded " *in laudem, gloriam, et honorem sancte et individue Trinitatis, Patris et Filii et Spiritus sancti, gloriossisime Virginis et beati Columbe abbatis, patroni nostri ecclesie parrochialis parrochie de Arryngrosk.*" This is a clear and satisfactory case of a medieval foundation dedicated to Columba.

53. DOLLAR. See *Liber Pluscardensis*, ed. F. J. H. Skene, Vol. I., p. 281 : "*Anglici . . . venientes apud ecclesiam de Doler, quae sancto Columbae sine medio pertinere dinoscitur,*" etc.

54. KINCARDINE-ON-FORTH. Here was " a croft of land of St. Colme."

55. INCHCOLM, Firth of Forth (on the Fife or Pictish side). The entry of David Camerarius, under 6th June (" *Hic et alius est a Columba sancto Abbate* "—*De Scotorum Fortitudine*, 1631, p. 153) clearly shows that he understood the saint of this island to be a different person from Columba: although Walter Bower, writing in the fourteenth century (*Scotichronicon*, Bk. V., chap. 38, ed. W. Goodall, Vol. I., pp. 286-7), thought that Columba was the patron. Bower as abbot of the monastery would naturally be inclined to give credence to an opinion that connected his house with so illustrious a patron. It is not improbable that this may be a foundation of Colman, Bishop of Lindisfarne (661-4), in the days of Anglian northward expansion, to which a halt was called by Brude Mac-Bile's great victory at Dunnichen (20th May, 685). The remarkable Celtic oratory or cell at Inchcolm (see Fig. 58), has often been described. See MacGibbon and Ross, *Ecclesiastical Architecture*, Vol. II., pp. 309-11. It is by no means of the most ancient type, being covered in with a true vaulted roof, and may be as recent as the eleventh or twelfth century. Two sculptured stones of Anglian type remain here (Fig. 57).

III.—Church site in the Anglian Kingdom of Bernicia.

56. CRAMOND, Midlothian. This is included by Dr. Reeves among Columba's churches. But the *New Statistical Account*, Vol. I., p. 604, merely says that the church had two altars, one dedicated to the Virgin Mary and the other to St. Columba (*cf. Reg. Great Seal*, 1660-68, No. 323). St. Columba's altar is explained by the fact that Cramond was a mensal church of Dunkeld. For *Sanct-Columbis-Well* "between the lands of the commonty of Cramond and the beach," see *Registrum Magni Sigilli*, 1593-1608, No. 1146.

IV.—Church sites in the Britonic Kingdom of Strathclyde.

57. DRYMEN, Stirlingshire. St. Columba's Church, but St. Colm's Fair. Mr. Scott, *Pictish Nation* (pp. 256, 554, 380) considers this to be a genuine foundation of Columba among the Britons. See *supra*, p. 29, note 1.

58. KILMACOLM, Renfrewshire. There is no evidence of any kind connecting this church with Columba.

59. LARGS, Ayrshire. This church is said to have been dedicated to St. Columba, but St. Colm's Fair was held here.

60. GREAT CUMBRAE. "Ane kirk callit Sanct Colmis Kirke." See Deane Munro's *Description of the Western Isles*, A.D. 1549, in *Miscellanea*

Scotica, Vol. II., p. 114. On Little Cumbrae is the chapel of St. Vey or Baya, who lived as a hermit here; see Forbes, *Kalendars*, pp. 276-7.

61. KIRKCOLM, Wigtown. In this parish there are two wells named after St. Columba, together with the site of St. Mary's Chapel, Kilmorie, and St. Mary's Well, both on St. Mary's Croft; the site of St. Bride's Church, and St. Bride's Well, East Kirkbride; and the site of Chapel Donnan, Broomhill. Of Kirkcolm itself, the site also alone remains. At Chapel Donnan, two sculptured cross-slabs were found, and at Kilmorie Chapel an ornate Celtic cross-slab formerly stood (Fig. 59). See *Ancient Monuments Commission, Report on Wigtown*, pp. 33-5, with authorities cited. That Columba was ever in this locality is highly improbable: on the other hand, the district seems to be intimately associated with early Strathclyde Christianity, as the site Chapel Donnan suggests (*cf. supra*, p. 39, note 1). The neighbouring parish is Kirkcowan, probably named after St. Comgan of Turriff, in Aberdeenshire, who also seems to have emanated from *Candida Casa*. See my *Origins of Christianity in Aberdeenshire*, pp. 31-2: but *cf.* Watson, *Celtic Place Names of Scotland*, p. 164. The use of " kirk " in these place-names indicates Anglian influence after the absorption of *Candida Casa* into the diocese of York (see *supra*, pp. 30-1).

62. CAERLAVEROCK, Dumfries: St. Columba's Chapel and Well, Probably this is a Celto-Norse or a medieval dedication. The name Kilblain or Kirkblain, which occurs at Caerlaverock, suggests that the Christianity of this neighbourhood was derived from the Britonic monastery and missionary centre of Kingarth (see Watson, *op. cit.*, pp. 164-5).

One of the most striking and best documented instances of the wrongful ascription of a church to St. Columba is furnished by the case of Tarbat in Ross-shire. In 1529 this is " the church of St. Colman situated in the place called Tarbert," see *Origines Parochiales*, Vol. II., part II., p. 434. St. Colman's name is preserved in that of the local harbour, which is Portmahomack—in the eighteenth century *Portmaholmack*, see *Old Statistical Account*—i.e., *Port-mo-Cholmaig*, Colm's port: the saint's name, Colman or Colm, with the honorific prefix *-mo* and the endearing suffix *-oc*. In the village is *Tobar-ma-Chalmag*, Colman's Well. Yet in medieval charters the name of the place was ignorantly latinised as *portus Columbi*, see *Macfarlane's Geographical Collections*, Vol. I., p. 215.

Quite possibly St. Colman or Colm of Tarbat is the same person as St. Colm of Buchan and Caithness. It is easy to imagine how he may have touched at Tarbatness on his voyage between Wick and Aberdour (see *supra*, p. 37, note 4).

The Archæological Evidence.

(For the classification of the Pictish Sculptured Stones, see pp. 79-80).

Against the " Columban myth" the appeal lies not merely from the distortions of medieval fabulists to a re-examination of the ancient records; it lies also to the face of Pictland, upon which archæological evidence still abounds that has its own story to tell. For the area served by the Brito-Pictish Church—the Church of Ninian and Kentigern—is also precisely the area in which occurs the remarkable symbolism of the early Christian Pictish sculptured stones. These symbol-marked stones, with or without the addition of the Christian cross, are found in great abundance all over eastern Pictland, from the Forth to the Shetlands, but never in the Scotic region west of Drumalban. Such outlying examples as occur beyond this dividing range—the Pabbay stone, the Benbecula stone, and the Skeabost stone in Skye[1]—are situated beyond the limits of old Dalriada; and one of them at least—the Pabbay stone—occurs at a known Pictish religious site. Mr. Romilly Allen has pointed out that only two symbol-stones occur within a hundred miles of Iona.[2] The symbols are not found in Strathclyde or Bernicia,[3] but were evidently a purely Pictish development —the original centre of dispersion, as the distribution and numbers of the earliest class of these monuments suggests, being apparently in Aberdeenshire.[4] The distribution of these early Christian stones is a point of cardinal significance. So far back as 1851 it was recognised by Sir Daniel Wilson, who pointed out that "no example occurs within the ancient

[1] See Figs. 18-21.

[2] *The Early Christian Monuments of Scotland*, by J. Anderson and J. Romilly Allen, Part II., p. 14. " The system of the symbolism was a general one, applicable to the whole area of the eastern side of Scotland, from Shetland to the Forth,"—*ibid.*, Part I., p. cx. *Cf.* Part II., p. 108.

[3] A solitary example of the oldest class occurs on a rock surface at Anwoth in Kirkcudbright-shire. So also there is a single "outlier" within the limits of Bernicia—a stone of Class I., found on the slope of the Castle Rock of Edinburgh. (On the subject of these isolated examples, see remarks by Dr. John Stuart, *The Sculptured Stones of Scotland*, Vol. II., Preface, p. 5.) The distribution of the oldest stones is an important point in determining their date. As in late Roman times the Picts are known to have occupied, or at least controlled, the whole of Caledonia up to Hadrian's Wall, it would appear to follow, from the absence of symbols in Bernicia, Strathclyde and Dalriada, that the oldest symbol stones must date subsequently to the formation of these kingdoms by Anglian, Britonic, and Scotic immigration in the sixth century.

[4] *Early Christian Monuments of Scotland*, Part I., p. cv. ; Part II., pp. 13, 108. See also F. C. Diack in *Loch Kinnord*, by the Rev. J. G. Michie, IInd edition, p. 162.

K

limits of Dalriada, or on the western coast in the vicinity of Ireland."[1]
Nor be it added, are the symbols found in Ireland itself, the country
whence Columba came. Mr. Romilly Allen, in gathering up the results
of his great national survey of these monuments, ventured a step further,
and boldly recorded his conclusion that their geographical distribution
"very decidedly negatives the theory that the symbols can have any connection with the Columban Christianity emanating from Iona."[2] We
may now go a step further yet, and point out that the distribution of the
symbols entirely concurs with the range of the pre-Columban church in
Pictland, of which the foundations were laid by St. Ninian's mission in the
early fifth century. There is no known other line of demarcation, racial,
cultural, or political, to which their distribution answers.

The question as to whether the earliest sculptured stones, which
display the incised symbols not in association with the cross, may not be
really pagan, has been much discussed. It seems to me that the arguments
so cogently marshalled by Dr. Joseph Anderson in favour of the Christian
origin of the symbols are unassailable.[3] In this connection Bishop G.
F. Browne has some very pertinent remarks. "The opinion," he writes,
"that the symbols are the distinguishing marks of the deities of pagan

---

[1] *The Archæology and Prehistoric Annals of Scotland*, 1st edition, p. 498.

[2] *Early Christian Monuments*, Part II., p. 14. Dr. Stuart, *Sculptured Stones of Scotland*,
Vol. II., Preface, p. 4, note 2, acutely observes that "neither at Dunkeld nor Brechin—two religious
establishments of Scotic foundation—have stones with the symbols been discovered ; while they are
found around neighbouring sites, some of them of an earlier date, as at Monifieth, Kingoldrum,
Meigle, and Aberlemno." *Cf.* also *ibid.*, p. 34.

[3] "Although none of these symbols are ever associated on the monuments of Class I. with any
of the common symbols of the Christian faith, they are used in association with the cross and with
other symbols and symbol pictures familiarly known as Christian on the decorated monuments of
Class II. They were therefore plainly capable of expressing or supplementing Christian symbolism,
and it is highly probable that the sense in which they appeared on the later monuments was also
the sense in which they appeared on the earlier. If this be so, they could never have been distinctively pagan. It is difficult, on the one hand, to imagine a system of paganism so restricted in
its area and yet so productive of symbolism. No known system of paganism in Europe has
exhibited anything like the fertility of symbolic expression which characterises this limited area of
Scotland. And on the other hand, although it is true that in the first ages of the Church in Rome
a few of the pagan pictorial symbols were taken and adapted to Christian significations, it can
hardly be supposed that the Christian teachers anywhere could possibly have tolerated the trans-
ference of an entire system of heathen symbolism to Christian uses "—*Early Christian Monuments*,
Part I., pp. xxxix-xl ; see also *ibid.*, p. cxi. The reader should also consult the same writer's
Scotland in Early Christian Times, Second Series, pp. 132-3, 180-9. "All their associations are of
Christian character. When they stand alone there is no suggestion of paganism connected with
them. They have never been found in associations which are definitively pagan. They are often
found associated with the emblems of the Christian faith, and there is therefore no warrant for
assigning to them a character which is not suggested either by their nature or their associations "
(p. 188, footnote).

faiths is difficult to maintain. It is much easier to maintain that they were not symbols against which the Christian teachers had to wage a stern warfare of destruction. If they had remained, as they do in the Inverurie district, solitary, or grouped on rude stones, we might no doubt maintain with much probability that they were the symbols of a paganism abandoned and in course of time forgotten. But when we find the Christian cross incorporated with them, at first tentatively and sparsely, and then increasingly prominent, till in the fully developed sculptures the cross is by far the most important and beautiful feature of the sculpture, we seem bound to believe that there had never been anything druidical, gentile, diabolic, in their meaning and use." [1]   But for our present purpose this question is really not of essential importance. The point which matters is that the symbols, whether pagan in their origin or not, were at all events capable in their entirety of bearing a Christian meaning, as their association with the cross and other Christian emblems on so many of the monuments shows. Even the earliest stones, with incised symbolism and no cross, occur again and again at definitely Christian sites. I know of at least fifteen such cases in the district between the Dee and the Spey alone. And even where the primitive incised symbol-stone stands now unassociated with any ascertained religious site, we must remember that all knowledge of an early wattled or timber church may well have long since perished.[2]

Thus the distribution of these symbols constitutes a differentiation between the early Christian monuments on both sides of Drumalban.[3] But the distinction is not confined to the symbol-stones. In eastern Pictland the type of earliest monumental cross, whether associated with the symbols or not, is always a cross graven on a slab; on the west, in the Dalriadic district, while slab crosses are occasionally found,[4] the typical cross, throughout the whole period of Celtic art, is the free-standing cross, of which the great High Cross of St. Martin at Iona [5] has become the stock example. The occasional free-standing crosses found on the eastern side of the watershed—such as those at Dupplin and

[1] *Antiquities in the Neighbourhood of Dunecht*, pp. 136-7.

[2] "On the whole, it is quite obvious that the associations of the monuments are Christian rather than pagan"—J. Romilly Allen in *Early Christian Monuments*, Part II., p. 19.

[3] Dr. Anderson, *Early Christian Monuments*, Part I., p. ciii, comments on "the remarkable fact" that "Scotland is divided into two monumental areas—one lying east of Drumalban and north of the Forth, which contains monuments of the whole three classes, and the other lying west of Drumalban and south of the Forth, which contains monuments of the third and latest class only."

[4] As at Iona, see Fig. 60-1.

[5] Fig. 62.

Camuston,[1] and the group at St. Andrews—belong to a very late period, when Scotic and Anglian influences were coming to predominate in Pictland. Moreover even in the type of cross itself a certain distinction can be traced. In ancient Dalriada and the west generally, the form of cross is typically a shafted one; and often here the free-standing shafted cross assumes the characteristically Irish glorified form, with a halo round the head, as at St. Martin's Cross.[2] But in eastern Pictland, although the shafted cross is also found, and sometimes with a halo, we can distinguish also a series of crosses, equal armed and often wheeled like the most ancient Christian crosses in the country that still exist at or near *Candida Casa*. This series of equal-armed and often wheeled crosses—developed from the encircled Chi-Rho monogram [3]—can be traced from its original centre of dispersion at *Candida Casa* right through the area of Ninian's influence up the east coast as far as Bressay in Shetland.[4] Even in the shafted surface crosses of the east, which are always late, the shaft is often carefully differentiated from the cross proper,[5] which is really an equal-armed cross set on a pedestal—a type which occurs as a free-standing monument within the limits of Strathclyde.[6] These wheeled and often equal-armed slab, crosses of eastern Pictland seem to be quite different in their origin from the great shafted and glorified free-standing crosses of the west coast, the *provenance* of which is purely Irish. In the cross of glory the arms are always projected beyond the halo, whereas in the true wheel cross this never occurs. Again in the wheel cross the decoration is always clearly distinguished on cross and shaft, while on the cross of glory the whole monument is treated as a unit for decorative purposes. The

[1] For the Camuston Cross see Fig. 63. The form of the Dupplin cross head is distinctively Anglian. See *Ancient Monuments Commission, Report on Dumfries*, p. 247.

[2] The finest example of this beautiful form is the great Kildalton Cross in Islay (Fig. 64). This cross is purely Irish in all its main features. The form into which this type of cross ultimately developed in the Western Highlands in later times is shown by the Oronsay Cross, Fig. 65.

[3] The encircled Chi-Rho monogram in its simplest form is illustrated by the Kirkmadrine stones, Figs. 48 and 66. The next stage in its development is shown in the Whithorn stone, Fig. 67, where the sacred monogram is carved as a segmented cross within a circle, and resting on a shaft with expanded base. It is thus that the later long-shafted free cross with a circled head is evolved, as illustrated by a monument from the same neighbourhood, Fig. 68. This form of cross occurs elsewhere in Strathclyde, as at Monreith; St. Blane's, Bute; Millport, Great Cumbrae; and Kilbride, Arran. It seems to be distinctively Britonic, as it is common also in Wales, Cornwall, and the Isle of Man.

[4] As at Arbirlot (Fig. 69); Balnagowan, Aboyne (Fig. 70); Monymusk (Fig. 71); Botriphnie (Fig. 72); and Bressay (Fig. 73).

[5] As at Monymusk (Fig. 74), and Papil, Shetland (Fig. 75). The cross at Soroby, in Tiree (see p. 19, note 4), is of this type.

[6] See the example from Whithorn (Fig. 68). These crosses are of a late period.

essential difference between the Pictish and the Scotic crosses was clearly recognised so far back as 1866 by Dr. John Stuart, who then wrote:—" In Argyllshire and the Hebrides the early crosses are entirely different from those on the east coast of Scotland, and partake of the form and art of the Irish monuments; from which, and other facts already referred to, we conclude that the cross-slabs on the east coast were elaborated at an earlier period, and through an influence different from that which gave form to the Irish crosses." [1]

It is in fact clear that we have to deal with quite a different *facies* of early Christian monumental remains on either side of Drumalban. The significance of this circumstance in connection with the demarcation between the Pictish Church of Ninian and Kentigern, and the Scotic Church of Columba, appears to be unmistakable.

In Ireland, from which the Picts are so constantly asserted to have obtained their Christianity, a totally different series of early Christian monuments is found.[2] Except for their common Celtic general aspect, the Irish and the Pictish monuments are utterly distinct: on the other hand the Irish monuments are quite closely paralleled within the boundaries of ancient Dalriada. The oldest type of Christian monument in Ireland is formed by groups of upright cross-marked stones, arranged so as to form a burial enclosure—the old pagan stone circle, as it were, *sained* with the emblem of the new faith. Next to these in time come recumbent cross-bearing slabs, succeeded in their turn by free-standing crosses. The first two types are not found in Pictland[3]: the third type, as we have seen, occurs only rarely, and under special circumstances, indicative of Scotic or Anglian penetration; while on the other hand it is frequent in Dalriada. St. Martin's Cross at Iona, for example, very closely resembles the great Irish High Crosses of the tenth century. It belongs to a peculiarly Irish type of cross, with tall head and very short arms. On Inishail, an island in Loch Awe, a cross of this type occurs, graven on a slab; while at Kilmartin, in the same neighbourhood, and at Keills in Knapdale,[4] the same form of cross occurs free standing. All these monuments are within the confines of what was once Dalriada.

---

[1] *Sculptured Stones of Scotland*, Vol. II., Preface, p. 45. In the *Early Christian Monuments of Scotland* this difference has to a large extent been forgotten.

[2] The best short account of the early Christian monuments of Ireland will be found in A. C. Champneys, *Irish Ecclesiastical Architecture*, Chap. V, part 2.

[3] In Strathclyde occurs a remarkable group of recumbent cross-bearing slabs of quite Irish type: no less than 29 examples at Govan, 1 at Inchinnan, and 1 at St. Blane's, Bute—the last mentioned site being on the borderland of Dalriada.

[4] Fig. 76.

Another feature which distinguishes the Pictish from the Irish monuments is the extreme rarity of the Crucifixion on the former. When found it is always on crosses of late or Scotic type,[1] and it is very common on the West Highland crosses of the later medieval period.[2] In Irish manuscript designs the Crucifixion is constantly shown, while on the other hand nothing is ever found that might have suggested the great decorated slab-crosses or the recondite symbolism of Pictland. The surface decoration found on Pictish monuments is in general more delicate than that of the Irish stones. But the point in which the Pictish monuments are most distinguished from all other manifestations of Celtic art is in their superb animal portraiture.[3] "The animals that are most faithfully represented are horses, deer, and dogs in action; and in the portrayal of such familiar animals there is displayed a certain accentuation of their distinctive characteristics, and a feeling for form and movement, which is very remarkable. Even the grotesque and fabulous animals are often rendered with spirited and suggestive effects of intensity of effort and malignity of character. When we consider the rigid conventionalism of the ornamental sculpture worked into patterns, and contrast it with the grace and freedom and vitality of the animal sculpture, we see that the last is something very different in quality from the work of the Irish illuminators. The feeling for animal characteristics which pervades the sculpture of the Scottish monuments is so unlike anything elsewhere found in the art of the time, that it must necessarily be regarded as an outcome of racial aptitude—an artistic development of the Pictish character superadded to the inspiration received from the ecclesiastical manuscripts." [4]

The whole question of the early Christian monuments of Scotland is one of great complexity, and the pitfalls of premature generalisation are obvious. But to me it seems that a long and a sure stride forward will have been made when once it is generally realised that the special character of the Pictish monuments is interwoven with the fact that they are the artistic product, not of a mere westward extension (through Dalriada) of Irish Christianity, but of a separate and older national Church, having its own *ethos*, traditions, organisation, personnel, and sources of supply.

[1] As on the Kirkcolm and Camuston Crosses, Figs. 59, 63. It appears also on the door of Brechin round tower, Fig. 24.

[2] As on the Oronsay Cross, Fig. 65.

[3] Figs. 75, 77, 78.

[4] Dr. Joseph Anderson in *Early Christian Monuments of Scotland*, Part I., pp. lxiv-v; *cf.* also p. lxxxi. Of the Irish figure carving Mr. Champneys remarks (*Irish Ecclesiastical Architecture*, p. 87) that it "seems to be the work of men possessing technical skill, but with a natural aptitude and taste rather for ornamental patterns (in which they are altogether excellent) than for producing representations of living things, whether plants, animals, or men."

Notes on the Illustrations.

The Classification of the Pictish Sculptured Stones.

Comparative study of these monuments has shown that they fall into an older, a middle, and a newer class.

Class I. The stones are natural boulders or monoliths, unshaped and undressed, and the sculpture consists of incised symbols sometimes ornamented with curved or spiral lines. Examples, Figs. 16, 18, 19, 20, 29, 30, 31 (left hand stone), 77, 78.

Class II. The stones are now for the most part slabs more or less carefully shaped and dressed, and bear in addition to the symbols a cross of Celtic type. The sculpture is usually in relief, and the cross and symbols are often richly decorated. Figure groups appear in the later specimens. Examples, Figs. 14, 17, 28, 31 (right hand stone), 53, 54, 74.

Class III. On these stones the symbols have disappeared, and we find merely the cross in relief, often of a highly enriched pattern, and associated in many cases with elaborate figure groups. Examples, Figs. 55, 73, 75. (One of the finest examples of the enriched cross-slab without either symbols or figure sculpture is the great Kinnord stone, shown in the Frontispiece of my *Origins of Christianity in Aberdeenshire.*)

Of course, no absolute date can be assigned to any of these monuments, and there was doubtless much overlapping between the different groups and in different districts. A great deal clearly depended on the presence in a given locality of soft rocks, such as sandstone, suitable for carving into the more elaborate monuments. This, doubtless, is partly the reason why the district betwixt Dee and Spey, with its hard granitic and schistose rocks, is pre-eminently the home of monuments of Class I., while in the adjoining districts of the Mearns and Moray Class II. is predominant. Still, it has been found possible on sound evidence to fix the approximate periods of the three groups as follows :—

Class I., prior to about 800.

Class II., about 800-1000.

Class III., from about 1000 to the extinction of the native Celtic style by intruded medieval (Anglo-Norman) art in the 12th and 13th centuries.

Some of the plain incised crosses without enrichment, such as Figs. 33, 35, 50, 70, may be of early date. The oldest type of all is the equal-armed and wheeled form, with or without a shaft, shown in Figs. 71 and 72, and in a more developed example in Fig. 73. This type of cross in Ireland is assigned by Professor Macalister to the eighth century or earlier. In Scotland, as I have shown, the type seems to be derived from St. Ninian's monastery at *Candida Casa,* whence also it probably spread to Ireland.

As to the symbolism, despite all guesses, its meaning remains shrouded in what Dr. Joseph Anderson has well described as "obstinate impenetrability" (*Scotland in Early Christian Times,* Second Series, p. 175). The names applied to the symbols, such as "elephant," "double disc and Z-rod," and so forth, are purely descriptive and conventional. The symbols have also been found on objects of bone and metal, and on the walls of caves.

A striking feature about the more ancient monuments is the artless beauty of their unshapen outlines. Nothing could be more absolutely satisfying to the eye than the profiles of the stones at Figs. 16, 20, 29, 30, 31 (left hand stone) and 74.

The standard work on the whole subject is *The Early Christian Monuments of Scotland,* by J. Romilly Allen and J. Anderson, 1903 : but the earlier work of Dr. John Stuart, *The Sculptured Stones of Scotland,* 2 vols., 1856 and 1867, will always be of permanent value. In the following notes the former work is referred to as *ECM,* the latter as *Stuart.*

Fig. 1. Map of Ireland, to illustrate Columba's Life.

Fig. 2. Map showing the monastic sites at Iona, with inset sketch-map of the island. (Place names are spelt as in the Ordnance Survey.)

Fig. 3. A page of the Cathach. See p. 6, note 3. The standard account of this famous manuscript is the exhaustive discussion by Professor H. J. Lawlor in *Proc. Royal Irish Academy,* Vol. XXXIII, Section C, No. 11 (pp. 241-436)—with a description of the shrine by E. C. R. Armstrong, and palæographical notes by Professor W. M. Lindsay.

The Cathach is now preserved in the Library of the Royal Irish Academy, within a beautiful silver and gold *cumdach* or shrine, which (as we learn from an inscription on its base) was made to enclose the greatly venerated book at the order of Domnall MacRobartaigh, *Coarb* of Kells (*circa* 1062-1098). The book is incomplete : it contains 58 consecutive leaves, all more or less damaged, and includes the Psalter continuously from Ps. XXX., v. 10, to Ps. CV., v. 13. There is evidence that the codex was already in this imperfect state when the costly shrine was made to enclose it in the latter half of the eleventh century. The manuscript is written throughout in one hand. Evidences of haste are visible in careless errors and in other ways; and there are signs that the scribe was hard put to obtain vellum. It is also clear that the manuscript was not compared with the exemplar after it had been transcribed. Dr. Lawlor concludes that the writer "was a penman of more than average excellence, who could not write rapidly, but who was working at unusually high pressure when he made this transcript of the

Psalter" (p. 250). All the foregoing evidence is, of course, thoroughly in accordance with the circumstances under which Columba is said to have made his surreptitious copy of St. Finbar's codex.

The handwriting is a small flowing half-uncial script approximating to a minuscule. It is a script in which—to quote Professor Lindsay—"the formal book hand of the time seems to have been modified so as to enable the writer to get through his task more quickly and to use less parchment" (p. 397). Palæography, concludes Professor Lindsay, "offers no reason for disbelief of the tradition which assigns the Cathach to the pen of St. Columba" (p. 403). A later hand has embellished the capitals with colouring : but the manuscript is a plain one of no intrinsic value, and the special care taken in the eleventh century to preserve it in a costly *cumdach* shows how ancient was its reputation for peculiar sanctity. As Dr. Reeves justly remarks (*Adamnan*, 1874, p. lxxxvi), "its claim to be considered in the handwriting of St. Columba derives some weight from the great veneration in which it was formerly held, notwithstanding the total absence of decoration."

An analysis of the text shows that its base is the Gallican version of the Hieronymian recension, with some admixture of old Latin readings ; and study of its variations leads to the conclusion that it "may be dated with high probability not later than the middle of the seventh century, and that it had some connection with Iona" (p. 292). Thus all available lines of evidence, as far as they can be explored, converge in pointing to the probable genuineness of the manuscript as the transcript of St. Finbar's codex that led to the battle of Cooldrevny and Columba's exile to Iona. The monastery of Kells, where the manuscript was preserved when the shrine was made for it, became the chief house of the Columban order in Ireland in the ninth century, when Iona was devastated by the Vikings : it would thus be a most likely place for Columba's relics to be carried to for safety.

The page illustrated is folio 56, the recto side, after Lawlor's facsimile. It shows part of Psalm XCVI. and the beginning of Psalm XCVII. (our Psalms XCV. and XCVI.). The first three lines of Psalm XCVII read thus :—

> " CANtate d̄no canticum nouum
> Quoniam mirabilia fecit ÷
> Saluabit sibi dextera eius : et bracchium s̄ctm eius ÷ "

The name Cathach (pronounced *Caah*) means "Battler." It is thus explained in O'Donnell's *Life of Columcille* (1532), in the account of Cooldrevny (§ 178, ed. A. O'Kelleher and G. Schoepperle, p. 183). "The *Cathach* for a sooth is the name of that book by reason whereof the battle was fought. And it is covered with silver under gold. And to open it is not lawful. And if it is borne thrice sunwise round the host of the clan of Conall when they go into battle, they come back safe in triumph. And it is in the bosom of a successor or a cleric that is so far as maybe without mortal sin, that the *Cathach* should be borne around the host."

L

Fig. 4.   Iona, view showing the old and the new monastic sites.   See Appendix I.   This photograph is taken looking north-eastward from the *Blar Buidhe,* the high ground to the west of *Releig Orain* (see Map, Fig. 2).   In the foreground is *Releig Orain,* with its ruined Romanesque church (see p. 55), and behind it is the restored Benedictine Abbey, which, about 1507, became the Cathedral Church of the Isles.   To the left of the Cathedral may be seen the roofless conventual buildings.   On the extreme left of the picture the house Clachanach is visible, and the probable site of Columba's monastery is on the flat, shoreward plain beyond.

Fig. 5.   "St. Columba's Pillow."   This is a water-worn stone, 1 foot 7 inches long, 1 foot 3½ inches wide, and 4½ inches thick, on which a shafted cross of glory is sculptured in relief.   The shape of the boulder seems unsuited for monumental purposes, and it has been conjectured that this may actually be the stone used by St. Columba as a pillow.   Adamnan, in the last chapter of his *Life,* tells us that in his own time the pillow stone was carefully preserved beside the saint's grave.   It is easily understood how the cross may subsequently have been carved upon the stone to mark its special sanctity. The stone, now preserved in the Cathedral, was found about 150 yards from *Cladh-nan-duiseart,* that is, in the immediate vicinity of the site of Columba's monastery.

Fig. 6.   Map of Celtic Scotland.   The Ninianic site at Fochabers, marked conjectural on the map, was St. Ninian's in the Enzie—see Jervise, *Epitaphs and Inscriptions,* Vol. I., pp. 277-9.   For the Ninianic site at Dunnottar see my *Dunnottar Castle,* IInd ed., pp. 2-3.

In 1909, Professor W. J. Watson expressed doubt as to the evidence that St. Ninian had laboured north of the Grampians (see *Trans. Gaelic Society of Inverness,* Vol. XXVII., p. 160).   In his recently published *Celtic Place Names of Scotland,* pp. 295-6, this doubt has crystallised into a virtual refusal to admit that any of the Scottish commemorations of St. Ninian date back to old Celtic times.   Professor Watson points out that in the churches ascribed to him "his name never appears in its native form;   what appears is either the latinised form or a Gaelic form derived therefrom through Scots vernacular.   He is thus a notable exception to the rule that though the name of a native saint may be found latinised in a Latin document, it is the native name, handed down by tradition, that appears in commemorations.   It is also notable that we have no record of any personal name formed from his name with *maol* or *gille* prefixed;   nor have I met an instance of a fair being named after him.   All this points to a tradition broken and subsequently revived";   and Professor Watson finds the explanation in a supposed "booming" of the Ninianic cult by David I. for the purpose of securing popular assent to his ecclesiastical innovations.   But surely this argument recoils on itself :   if David found it advisable to carry out his religious reforms under the patronage of St. Ninian, it clearly follows that Ninian must already have been a saint widely venerated among the Celtic population throughout the country—a circumstance all in favour of some, at least, of the churches bearing his name being older and not later than the twelfth century. I do not know a single vestige of evidence for Professor Watson's theory that David "ran" St. Ninian in opposition to St. Columba. On the contrary, there is evidence that such a proceeding would have been in flat contradiction to the settled policy of the House of Canmore. David's mother, the saintly Queen Margaret, from whom he inherited his church programme, had restored and endowed St. Columba's monastery at Iona. And in the reign of David's successor, Joceline of Furness, who was employed to write the lives of St. Ninian and St. Kentigern, in Chapter XXXIX. of the latter *Life,* goes out of his way to pronounce a glowing eulogy upon Columba and his monastery : "*sanctus Columba abbas, quem Angli vocant Columkillum, doctrina et virtutibus mirabilis, futorum presagiis preclarus, utpote prophetico spiritu plenus, in illo glorioso cenobio quod in insula Yi construxerat degens,*" etc.

On the special question of the dedications, that there is a strong element of truth in Dr. Watson's view is beyond dispute : it is absurd to assume that the numerous churches bearing Ninian's name—greatly exceeding those ascribed to Columba—could have been founded by the saint in person. But Professor Watson ignores some undoubted evidence linking Ninianic sites in Pictland with the Celtic Church. For example, St. Ninian's chapel-site at Methlick bears the name Andet or Annat (*andóit, annáid*), which is invariably associated with a founder's church. This word is a well-known Celtic church term, both in Ireland and in Scotland ; and Professor Watson himself remarks (*op. cit.,* p. 251) that in Scotland "wherever there is an Annat there are traces of an ancient chapel or cemetery, or both : very often, too, the Annat adjoins a fine well or clear stream." In an earlier work (*Place Names of Ross and Cromarty,* Introduction, p. lxiv.) Professor Watson had remarked of the Scottish Annats : "they are of great antiquity, indicating, doubtless, the earliest Christian settlements in their particular districts." Yet he now proceeds to dismiss Andet of Ninian at Methlick in the following summary words (*Celtic Place Names of Scotland, p.* 252) : "it appears often on record, and had a chapel dedicated to St. Ninian, but this is plainly a secondary dedication." Why? And if so, whence Andet? His attempt (*op. cit.,* pp. 318-20, 324) to meet this self-created difficulty by connecting the perfectly definite and well documented Annat of St. Ninian at Methlick with St. Murdebur of Tarves, mentioned in the *Martyrology of Oengus,* seems to me in the highest degree forced and unlikely. The Ninianic site associated with the old Celtic religious name cannot be disposed of in this cavalier fashion.

Again, surely the presence at Ninianic church sites of early symbol or cross-marked stones—as at Arbirlot, see Fig. 69 (not to speak of the documentary evidence of a Celtic monastery there)—is evidence linking such sites with the Celtic Church. Indeed, one of the great weaknesses in Professor

Watson's handling of the church sites seems to me to be his complete ignoring of the archæological evidence.

Fig. 7.   A and B.   Views of Dunadd, the first capital of the Scots in Scotland, taken from the north-west and north-east respectively.   These photographs well bring out the twin-topped site, and its relation to the River Add and the surrounding plain.

Fig. 8.   Plan of Dunadd.   The arrangement of the hill-fort, as shown on plan, with its series of enclosures, gives an impression of spaciousness which must be corrected by reference to the scale.

Fig. 9.   Dunadd :   view of the inner face of the wall at the entrance to the enclosure A, showing the massive and regular character of the dry-built masonry.

Fig. 10.   Dunadd :   entrance to enclosure F, looking out.   This view strikingly reveals the commanding nature of the site.

Fig. 11.   Dunadd :   the famous incised carving of a boar.   It is 21 inches long, and is placed (at the point marked on plan, Fig. 8) between the foot mark and the cup.   The back of the animal has disappeared through weathering, but the portions of the drawing which are preserved reveal the work of a consummate artist.   This feeling for animal portraiture is a Pictish rather than a Scotic characteristic (see p. 78).

Fig. 12.   Dunadd :   Some of the querns found in the course of excavation. The scale is shown by the 3-foot rule in front.

Fig. 13.   Dunadd :   a selection from the relics found during the excavations (not to uniform scale).   No. 1 is a fragment of a large pitcher in coarse red, wheel-made ware.   No. 2 is one of eight iron tools, varying from 4 to $5\frac{1}{2}$ inches long, of unknown use.   No. 3 is an iron ring, 5 inches in diameter.   No. 4 is a bone comb, $2\frac{1}{2}$ inches long.   Nos. 5-8 are iron spearheads.   No. 9 is an iron knife-blade.   Nos. 10-11 are bronze pins, $3\frac{1}{2}$ inches long.   No. 12 shows three glass beads, the lower one clear green, $\frac{1}{2}$ inch in diameter, the middle one blue with whitish stripes, the top one of a dark blue tint.   Nos. 13, 17, 18, 20 and 21 show clay crucibles, No. 20 with traces of bronze adhering to its interior.   Nos. 14 and 23 are iron combs, probably for carding.   No. 15 is a disc of green slate, $1\frac{5}{8}$ inches in diameter, incised with the words I[N]NOMINE (see p. 17, note 2).   No. 16 is a carved greenstone ball, $2\frac{3}{4}$ inches in diameter, of Pictish type.   No. 19 is a stone mould, and No. 22 a mould in clay.   No. 24 is a piece of slate, on which has been scratched the working drawing for a brooch.   No. 25 is a piece of slate with incised ornamental designs.

It may be noted that crucibles similar to those from Dunadd were obtained in the excavations at Nendrum.   At the latter place were also found three stone holders for such crucibles.   "These were nodules of stone," writes Mr. H. C. Lawlor, "in which a recess had been chiselled out to fit the crucible. When the metal was brought to the molten stage, the holder was lifted out of the fire by tongs, with the crucible firm in the recess, and the metal poured into stone moulds. Without the stone holders, the tongs would probably have broken the crucible, or it would likely have capsized in the fire. To secure safety, the recess in the holder was made to fit the crucible exactly, and grip it. The holders are polychromatic and highly glazed, through the action of heat with the molten metal, which in places still adheres"—*The Monastery of St. Mochaoi of Nendrum*, p. 142. On this Mr. A. O. Curle comments (*Scottish Historical Review,* Vol. XXII., No. 88, p. 299): "This does not seem a very easy process to accomplish. Though crucibles have been found in various early sites in Scotland, stones hollowed to fit them have not been found so far, but Traprain Law yielded a small pair of crucible tongs obviously to be used directly on the crucible."

As to the wheel-turned pitcher, at Nendrum the introduction of wheel-made pottery is assigned to the seventh or eighth century, and no glazed ware seems to occur before the Norman invasion (twelfth century). See Lawlor, *op. cit.,* pp. 161-2, 171, 173.

Fig. 14. A and B. Front and back views of a splendid Pictish sculptured symbol stone of Class II., at St. Moluag's foundation of Rosemarkie. In its present mutilated condition this freestone slab measures 8 feet 6 inches high, and must originally have been fully a foot taller. The front shows in its upper portion a plain equal-armed cross with recessed angles, enclosed in a mass of interlaced work, while the lower portion is covered with convoluted zoomorphic ornament. On the back, the upper part of the slab displays the "crescent and V-rod" symbol thrice repeated (the uppermost one now being almost destroyed). Between the upper two crescents are a pair of grotesque beasts, each biting its own hind leg, while their tails run off into plait work. Above the lowest crescent the "double disc and Z-rod" symbol is introduced, and between these two symbols is inserted the "comb," while below the crescent what seem to be two "mirrors" are found. All these symbols are very highly enriched. In the middle part of the stone is an equal-armed cross of peculiar form (see Fig. 15), between four bosses, the whole being surrounded with plait work, and encased in a border of key-pattern enrichment. The lowest part of the slab is filled with key-pattern work. The edges also are richly ornamented with interlaced work and convoluted lacertine creatures, some of which have goats' heads. This stone was found, smashed into two pieces, in the floor of the old church.

Fig. 15. An enlarged drawing of the central cross-bearing panel on the back of the Rosemarkie stone, figured previously. This drawing well shows the extreme intricacy, richness, and elegance of the design. For a full description of this beautiful stone see *ECM,* part III., pp. 63-8.

In addition to this stone of Class II., four other fragmentary stones, all apparently of Class III., have been found at Rosemarkie. The fact that no stone of Class I. has turned up is quite in agreement with the known date (later sixth century) of the foundation of the early community. For the other four stones see *ECM,* part III., pp. 85-8.

Fig. 16. Symbol stone of Class I. recently discovered in the church-yard at Mortlach. It is a pillar-stone of psammitic gneiss, 5 feet 3 inches high. The upper symbol is the familiar "elephant," the lower one is hitherto unknown. The incised sculpturing is wrought with great precision and spirit. See my paper in *Proc. Soc. Ant. Scot.,* Vol. LX., pp. 274-5.

Fig. 17. Front and back views of the "Battle Stone" of Mortlach. This symbol stone of Class II. stands in the churchyard about 30 feet south-east of the spot where the other stone was recently found. The stone of gneiss is 5 feet 9 inches high above ground, and has in front a Celtic cross between two fish-like monsters facing each other on top, and a grotesque beast at the base, while on the other side are a bird, a serpent, an ox's head, and a horseman with his hound. In the illustration of the back of this stone in *ECM,* part III., p. 156, the bird is not shown, while in *Stuart* (Vol. I., plate XIV.) the eyes and nose of the ox's head are omitted. (See also note to Fig. 31.)

Fig. 18. The Skeabost Stone. This symbol stone of Class I. stands on the moor ½ mile north-east of Skeabost Bridge. It bears the crescent and V-rod and the "double disc and Z-rod," the latter turned up on end. Both symbols are ornamented. The stone is locally known as *Clach Ard.* See *Proc. Soc. Ant. Scot.,* Vol. XLIV., pp. 384-5.

Fig. 19. The Benbecula Stone (Class I.). It is a slab of granite, 3 feet long by 2 feet 6 inches broad, and on it are inscribed the "disc" symbol and the "rectangular" symbol, both simply yet effectively ornamented. The stone was found on the sea-shore at Strome Shunnamal, on the north-east side of the island, and close to the ruin of a building, perhaps a chapel. This stone is now preserved in the National Museum of Antiquities of Scotland, Edinburgh. See *Proc. Soc. Ant. Scot.,* Vol. VIII., p. 285.

Fig. 20. The Pabbay Stone (Class I.). This is a dioritic monolith, 3 feet high. On it are incised an equal-armed cross with stopped terminals, resting on the "crescent and V-rod" symbol, while below the latter is the "flower" symbol. Both symbols are ornamented.

Fig. 21. An outline drawing showing more clearly the carving on the Pabbay Stone. This monument lies in St. Moluag's churchyard (see p. 28, note 2).

It is noteworthy that the foregoing three outlying examples of the Pictish symbol stones all belong to the oldest (Class I.) type. The same is true of the other outliers, at Edinburgh Castle and at Anwoth in the Stewartry of Kirkcudbright. For the probable significance of this fact see p. 73, note 3

Fig. 22. A and B. Elevation and section of the Abernethy round tower. This tower—"a stately hollow Pillar" as Sandy Gordon quaintly described it (*Itinerarium Septentrionale,* 1726, p. 164)—which stands on the edge of the old churchyard, is 72 feet in height and 8 feet in basal diameter, within walls 3 feet 6 inches thick. In the interior were six stages of wooden floors. The tower is well built of coursed masonry. The lower dozen courses —reaching to a height of about 14 feet—are of hard grey freestone in oblong blocks; but thereafter the tower is built in cubical, wide-jointed, buff-coloured freestone ashlar of pronouncedly Romanesque type. In both sections the stones are wrought to the curved outline of the tower. The doorway, which is encircled by a raised band, has inclined jambs in the Irish style, and an arched head cut out of a single stone. It is now about 3 feet above the ground level. The window in the second storey also has inclined jambs, and a triangular head cut out of one stone. The uppermost windows, four in number, show Irish influence persisting in their inclined jambs, but the nook-shafts and arch moulds are of distinctly Romanesque design. It is clear that the greater part of the tower has been rebuilt at a late period—probably about the end of the eleventh century, when Norman influence was making itself strongly felt. The lower portion may *possibly* date from the middle of the ninth century, the period favoured by Skene (*Celtic Scotland,* Vol. II., p. 309) on historical grounds. For the early religious history of Abernethy see Rev. D. Butler, *The Ancient Church and Parish of Abernethy.*

Fig. 23. A and B. Elevation and section of the Brechin round tower. This tower stands at the south-west angle of the thirteenth century Cathedral Church, to which it is now joined. To the base of the spire—which is an addition (following the original lines) of the later fourteenth century, *circa* 1351-73—the tower measures 86 feet 9 inches in height, and it is 7 feet 11 inches in internal basal diameter, the walls here being 3 feet 8 inches thick. Wooden floors divided the interior into seven storeys. The masonry is of red sandstone blocks, wrought to the curve but not regularly coursed, and occasionally with joggled or interlocking joints. There are two original windows, with flat heads and inclined jambs : the large rectangular openings on the uppermost floor are perhaps insertions. The doorway is about 6 feet above the present ground level, but 12 feet 2 inches above the internal founds of the tower, as revealed by excavation.

Fig. 24. The doorway of the Brechin round tower. No less in its ornamentation than in its structural features, this beautiful doorway—like the tower to which it admits—is completely Irish. Here, indeed, there is an utter absence of the Romanesque detail found in the Abernethy tower. The door shows the typically Irish inclined jambs and arched head wrought in a single stone. The double pellet-border on the raised band is found on the doors of some of the Irish towers and churches—as on the towers at Devenish (Fig. 25) and Disert Oengus : it also occurs on the High Crosses, as on Muireadhach's Cross at Monasterboice (dating probably from *circa* 924), and on the cross of glory at Drumcliff. (This pellet ornament is very constantly used in Ireland, where it survives into Romanesque and even later work—just as at Iona, in a region closely in touch with Irish influences, it is found on some of the late slabs.) Over the arched doorway is a sculpture of the Crucifixion : such representations are common in Ireland, but very rare in Pictland (see p. 78). Here at Brechin the Crucifixion has the characteristically Irish form, with the Saviour's legs uncrossed (see H. S. Crawford, *Handbook of Irish Carved Ornament,* p. 71, No. 142, and references). On the doorway of the tower at Donaghmore a Crucifixion, but with legs crossed, occurs in the same position as at Brechin : see illustration in Petrie, *Ecclesiastical Architecture of Ireland,* p. 410; also Champneys, *Irish Ecclesiastical Architecture,* Plate XXVI. The cleric on the left jamb carries a *bachuill* of typically Celtic form (see Fig. 36), while his companion is furnished with a "tau-cross," or T-shaped staff, a very rare occurrence : it is found on the cross of St. Tola at Disert O'Dea (Co. Clare), Ireland, dating probably from the twelfth century. At the foot of the doorway, outside the raised band, crouch two grotesque beasts, while at its upper end are two blank projecting blocks of stone, doubtless intended to be similarly carved. The doorway is 6 feet 7½ inches high.

For the early ecclesiastical history of Brechin see David Black, *The History of Brechin,* IInd edition, 1867; also *A Short History of Brechin Cathedral,* 1903, by the Rev. Walter W. Coats.

So far back as 1726 Alexander Gordon had dimly understood the significance of the presence of these Irish round towers in Pictland. "The vulgar Notion concerning these," he writes (*Itinerarium Septentrionale,* p. 165), " is that they are *Pictish,* and I should have easily rested in that Opinion, had I not been since that Time assured by a Gentleman of unquestionable Veracity, That some of the like Monuments are to be seen in *Ireland,* where the *Picts* never were settled."

Fig. 25. A and B. View and section of the tower at Devenish, a typical and perfect instance of an Irish round tower, showing how completely the outlying examples at Abernethy and Brechin correspond with the main group in Ireland. This tower contained five storeys with wooden floors, and is 84 feet 10 inches high to the apex : its internal diameter at the base is about 8 feet. The door is 9 feet above the ground level. On each upper floor one window is found, except in the top storey, where the usual four windows face the cardinal points. All the windows and the door have the usual inclined jambs.

About eighty of these round towers still survive in Ireland, in a greater or less degree of preservation. They date variously between the ninth and twelfth centuries, and the later examples—like the one at Abernethy—show pronounced, and sometimes (as at Kildare and Timahoe) very rich Romanesque details.   These towers are always found in connection with ecclesiastical sites, and were used as belfries, and as places of refuge where the clergy with their church furnishings and relics might find shelter amid the chronic conditions of warfare in early Ireland.   An analysis of their distribution reveals that the majority must have been built during the period of the Viking invasions.   "Heaven helps those who help themselves": and the round towers are thus the practical embodiment by the Irish clergy of the petition which in those dreadful days was added to the Church's Litany: *A furore Normannorum libera nos, Domine* !"   The most compact and recent study of these highly interesting structures will be found in Chapter IV. of Champneys' *Irish Ecclesiastical Architecture,* 1910: but the standard authority is still the famous work of Petrie, *The Ecclesiastical Architecture of Ireland,* IInd edition, 1845.   "Dr. Petrie's admirable work," as Sir Daniel Wilson strikingly remarked, in discussing the round towers (*Prehistoric Annals of Scotland,* IInd edition, Vol. II., p. 373), "has sufficed to sweep away the learned dust and cobwebs laboriously accumulated about the inquiry into their origin, and exhibits the value of patient investigation, and the logical deductions of a thoroughly informed mind, in contrast to the vague and visionary speculations of the fireside student."

Fig. 26.   Map showing Culdee stations in Scotland.

Fig. 27.   A and B.   Front and end views of the Monymusk Reliquary. This beautiful specimen of early Celtic Christian art dates probably from the eighth century.   It is a casket cut of solid wood, and plated with bronze and silver, which is adorned with enamel work, jewels, and engraved and stippled scroll and zoomorphic ornament.   Its dimensions are :—length, $4\frac{1}{4}$ inches ; breadth at base, 2 inches ; height, $3\frac{7}{8}$ inches.

Fig. 28.   Front and back views of the Stone of Deer.   This incised, cross-marked symbol stone of Class II. was formerly preserved among the Cistercian Abbey ruins, but has now disappeared—having apparently been broken up for building purposes (see *Stuart,* Vol. I., Plate XI., and Notices of the Plates, p. 6; also Vol. II., Appendix to the Preface, Additions and Corrections, p. xcvi.).   The symbols on the reverse side are the "crescent and V-rod," and the "rectangle," both enriched.   Assuming the cross to be contemporary with the symbols on the other side, then we have here a case of the "crescent and V-rod" in a reversed position, with the horns of the crescent pointing up.   But it is possible that the stone may have been turned upside down, and the cross added, at a later date.

Fig. 29.   Stone of Class I., with incised symbols, at St. Fergus' Church, Fetterangus.   It is of whinstone, 3 feet 8 inches long, and bears the "mirror case" (with ornate handle), and "triple disc and cross-bar" symbols, with a nondescript scrolled ornament above.

The churchyard of Fetterangus is of high antiquity.   It is mounded up,

M

like the churchyards at **Kildrummy**, St. Vigean's, and other early Christian sites.   The neighbourhood is rich in prehistoric remains, pointing to an early centre of population, such as would naturally attract a missionary.   To the west of the church, in the Den of Howie, is an earthwork; the site of a stone circle lies north-west of the latter; still further in the same direction was found a burial place with urns; north from the church are the remains of another stone circle; and flint arrowheads have been turned up at various points in the immediate vicinity.   Another group of early sites (urns, stone axes, stone whorls, flint arrowheads) lies further to the north, on the north flank of Shepherd's Hill, west of Nether Cabra.   See O.S. Map, 6 in., Aberdeenshire, Sheet XIII.   These evidences reveal the existence of a fixed population continuously since, at least, the beginning of the Bronze Age.

Fig. 30.   The Daviot symbol stone (Class I.).   This stone formerly stood at Newton of Mounie, to the north-east of the parish church of St. Colm, but is now preserved at Mounie Castle.   It is a whinstone slab, 2 feet 7 inches high, incised with the "crescent and V-rod," the "crescent" by itself, the "mirror," and the "comb."   The ends of the rod are floriated, the two crescents are enriched with curved lines, and the comb has an ornamental back.   The incision of the sculpturing is somewhat bolder than is usual in the Aberdeenshire stones.

Fig. 31.   Two fine sculptured symbol stones, now preserved under the Ancient Monuments Act, in the walls of the ruined medieval church of St. Fergus at Dyce.   The left hand stone (Class I.) is an unshaped boulder of greyish granite, 5 feet 6 inches long, and is incised with the "elephant" and "double disc and Z-rod" symbols.   This stone was found in the churchyard dyke.   The right hand stone is one of the five monuments of Class II., with Celtic cross and symbols, known to exist between the Dee and the Spey—the other four being the "Battle Stone" at Mortlach (Fig. 17), the "Maiden Stone" at Pitcaple, the Migvie Stone, the Formaston ogham Stone at Aboyne, and the Monymusk Stone (Fig. 74).   This splendid stone is roughly shaped and dressed, and carved in relief.   It is in granite, and measures 4 feet 6 inches high.   The cross is enriched with knot-work and spiral ornament. On the left of its shaft is the "crescent and V-rod," on the other side is the "mirror case," while below are respectively the "triple disc" and "the double disc and V-rod."   All these symbols are variously enriched.   This stone was dug up in the glebe.

Fig. 32.   Incised cross of unusual form, 6 inches high, at St. Fergus Church, Dyce.

Fig. 33.   Incised crosses of Celtic type at Dyce Church.   The largest stone is 2 feet 11 inches high.   The type of cross on the left-hand stone is found also in the eighth century at Clonmacnoise—see R. A. S. Macalister, *The Memorial Slabs of Clonmacnois,* Plate VI, Fig. 34.

It has been suggested (*Scottish Notes and Queries,* Third Series, Vol. III., No. 2, p. 24), that the early religious settlement at Dyce stood at Moss Fetach, nearly a mile to the south.   But the presence of the sculptured stones, no less than the superb scenic qualities of the site, strongly suggest that the medieval church occupies the original position selected by St. Fergus.   The very ancient inhabitation of Dyce is vouched for by the presence in the parish of one of the finest among the many stone circles in Aberdeenshire.

Fig. 34.   Sketch Map to illustrate the footsteps of "Drostan and his Three."

The crossing of the Moray Firth by early Celtic missionaries was quite usual :   church sites indicate that, besides "Drostan and his Three," St. Moluag, St. Curitan, St. Devenic, and St. Dubthac all laboured on both sides of the Firth.

For other Drostan sites see Forbes, *Kalendars of Scottish Saints,* p. 327 : but it may be questioned whether more than one saint are not involved.   The name of Drostan occurs in the tenth century minuscule inscription on the St. Vigean's Stone (*ECM,* part III., pp. 234-9).   There is nothing whatever to connect this with St. Drostan : but it is at least suggestive that this inscription should also contain another name that may very possibly be Fergus.   Professor Watson thinks this "more than likely" (*Celtic Place Names of Scotland,* p. 323).   The transliteration of the inscription—

> DROSTEN .
> IPEUORET
> ETTFOR
> CUS

—is not in doubt, but its translation is extremely obscure.   Mr. F. C. Diack's expansion of IPE into *In Pace* (*The Newton Stone and other Pictish Inscriptions,* p. 36) is a mere guess, and improbable at that : DNE for *Domine,* a single word, is not a sufficient parallel.

Fig. 35.   Incised cross slab from St. Colm's Church, Hoy, Orkney.

Fig. 36.   The *Bachuill Mor* or pastoral staff of St. Moluag.   This most remarkable relic of the early Celtic Church is still preserved in the custody of the Duke of Argyll.   See A. Carmichael, "The Barons of Bachuill" in *The Celtic Review,* Vol. V., pp. 356-75.   Sir Daniel Wilson, *Archæology and Prehistoric Annals of Scotland,* IInd edition, Vol. II., p. 478, describes it as "a plain curved staff, long since spoiled of its costlier ornaments, and retaining only a few of the rivets, and some fragments of the copper of its metal casing."   By the removal of the precious accretions with which the piety of later generations enshrined this venerated relic, the staff has reverted to the condition in which its owner used it.   Its length is 2 feet 10 inches. "It is a dull intelligence," truly remarks the Rev. A. B. Scott (*Transactions of the Scottish Ecclesiological Society,* Vol. III., part III., p. 307), "which is not startled by the survival of this pastoral staff into the twentieth century." (There is a coloured illustration, on a larger scale, in *Origines Parochiales Scotiae,* Vol. II, Part I, p. 163.)

Fig. 37. "St. Ninian's Bell," in the National Museum of Antiquities, Edinburgh. A good example of the iron hand bells used in the Celtic church. These bells are formed in two pieces, one bent round and riveted on to the other. Usually the bell was then dipped into melted bronze. In later times the bell ascribed to any notable saint became an object of extreme veneration, and for such bells costly and elaborate shrines were constructed, like the Guthrie and Kilmichael-Glasserie bell-shrines now preserved in the National Museum. For the use of the bell in Columba's monastery, besides the passage to which this is a note, see also *Adamnan,* Bk. II., Ch. XLII. and Bk. III., Ch. XIII.

Fig. 38. Map of Northumbria and her neighbours in the seventh century, to illustrate the Scotic mission.

(For *Figs. 39-44,* see Appendix V.)

Fig. 39. Early gravestone of Irish type from Lindisfarne. This stone measures $8\frac{1}{4}$ inches in height, and is incised with a cross having circles at the centre and at the three upper extremities, while the shaft rests upon a semi-circular pedestal. The stone has an arched head, and has been enclosed with a moulding. The inscription in Hiberno-Saxon lettering reads AEDBERECHT.

Figs. 40. Another of the Lindisfarne stones. In this fragmentary example the cross is enriched with the characteristic Celtic interlacement. Traces of an inscription in Hiberno-Saxon lettering remain.

Fig. 41. One of the group of early monumental slabs of Irish type from Hartlepool. This stone is of a rectangular shape, but the cross is of the same characteristic type as on the Lindisfarne stones. The inscription, here in runes, reads HILLDIGYTH.

Fig. 42. Two slabs at Clonmacnoise, showing very clearly the *provenance* of the Hartlepool-Lindisfarne group. The first one bears the inscription, in Irish minuscules : SUIBINE MCMAILAEHUMAI. His death is recorded under the year 890 : *Suibne MacMaelehumai, anchorita et scriba optimus Cluana mac Nois, dormivit—Annals of Ulster,* ed. W. M. Hennessy, Vol. I., p. 407. Thus the date of this type of stone is satisfactorily determined. The other stone is inscribed OR DO MAELBRIGTE, "Pray for Maelbrigte." The death of a Maelbrigte, Abbot of Clonmacnoise, is recorded in 891—*Annals of Ulster, ut supra,* p. 407.

See also Fig. 60, and note thereon. The standard work on the monuments at Clonmacnoise is Professor R. A. S. Macalister's *The Memorial Slabs of Clonmacnois.*

Fig. 43. A stone of later type from Lindisfarne. The general character of the monument recalls that of the earlier stones, but the cross has lost the distinctive "Clonmacnoise" form, and approximates closely to an ordinary Celtic type. "It is roughly drawn, and its interlacings are not accurately worked out : it also has rings intertwined, a feature which has been pronounced to be not earlier than the tenth century. But such rings occur in the Book of Durrow, *circa* 700, and are found in Scandinavian art of that period, and when the early shape of the cross is considered, there seems no reason why this cross should not be placed before the abandonment of the monastery in 875" (Peers). It is certainly quite impossible to date it from after the refounding of Lindisfarne by the Benedictines at the end of the eleventh century.

Fig. 44. A and B. Front and back view of one of the later Anglian stones at Lindisfarne. The front shows a plain Celtic cross, with sun and moon above and two adoring figures below, while on either side a hand demonstrates the Passion. The presence of the sun and moon on symbolical (as distinct from realistic) representations of the Passion is common in early art : they occur in the lowest panel on the back of the Ruthwell Cross (not shown in Fig. 46). On the reverse of the slab is a procession of armed figures, which strikingly recalls similar representations on the Pictish sculptured stones.

Fig. 45. A and B. The Bewcastle Cross, views from S.W and N.W. This superb monument of early Anglian Christianity stands in the churchyard of St. Cuthbert at Bewcastle, in Cumberland. The head of the cross has long since been broken off; in its mutilated condition the monument measures 14 feet 6 inches in height.

Fig. 46. A, B, C and D. The Ruthwell Cross, front, back, and left and right side views. These engravings show the shaft of the cross without its partly restored head : they also do not include the pedestal. In its present condition the total height of the monument is about 17 feet. This splendid cross, the most important early Christian monument in Scotland, is now preserved—after an unexampled and atrocious history of ill-treatment, misuse, and neglect—in an apsidal structure specially built on to the parish church in 1887; and its future safety is assured under the protection of the Ancient Monuments Act.

It is impossible, in the narrow compass of these notes, to attempt even an outline description of the Bewcastle and Ruthwell Crosses. Their importance from our special standpoint is dealt with in Appendix VI. A great bulk of literature has grown up around these two famous crosses : but the most exhaustive discussion of them both—alike in their historical, archæological, artistic, epigraphic, and linguistic bearings—will be found in the special Appendix to the *Royal Commission on Ancient Monuments, Report on Dumfriesshire,* pp. 219-86. Among subsequent notices reference may be made to O. M. Dalton, *East Christian Art,* pp. 65-9, 174; G. Baldwin Brown, *The Arts in Early England,* Vol. V ; and W. G. Collingwood, *Northumbrian Crosses of the Pre-Norman Age.* The reader may also consult Champneys, *Irish Ecclesiastical Architecture,* Appendix I. (pp. 216-25).

Fig. 47. A, B, C and D. Front, back, and left and right side views of the Coldingham stone, showing interlaced and zoomorphic ornament of the kind which the early Anglian Christians borrowed from their Celtic teachers. The monument, which is now preserved in the National Museum of Antiquities, Edinburgh, seems to be part of a cross-shaft. It is in red freestone, and measures 1 foot 3 inches high.

The history of Coldingham Priory has never been satisfactorily explored. The best works meantime are A. A. Carr, *History of Coldingham Priory,* 1836; W. King Hunter, *History of the Priory of Coldingham,* 1858; and A. Thomson, *Coldingham Parish and Priory,* 1908.

(For *Figs. 48-9,* see Appendix II.)

Fig. 48. The upper part of an early Christian monument at Kirkmadrine. This slab of indurated schist measures 6 feet 9 inches high. On the reverse side is incised the Chi-Rho monogram within a circle; while on the front (shown in the figure) are carved the Alpha and Omega, the Chi-Rho enclosed in a circle, and below this the incised inscription, in debased and ligatured Roman capitals :—

> HIC IACENT
> SCI ET PRAE
> CIPVI SACER
> DOTES IDES
> VIVENTIVS
> ET MAJORIVS

"Here lie the holy and excellent priests, Ides, Viventius, and Majorius." It should be noted that the Chi-Rho monogram is made with the Roman letter R, not the Greek P. The use of the word *sacerdos* may perhaps indicate that the persons commemorated were bishops. The monument dates probably from the later fifth century.

Fig. 49. The upper part of a stone at Whithorn. This is a slaty slab, about 4 feet 6 inches high, and bears the following incised inscription in debased Roman capitals :—

> TE D[OM]INVM
> LAVDAMV [S]
> LATINVS
> ANNORVM
> XXXV ET
> FILIA SVA
> ANNI V
> [H]IC SINVM
> FECERVNT
> NEPVS
> BARROVA
> DI

"We praise thee Lord. Latinus aged 35 years and his daughter aged 5 years. Here the descendants of Barrovad made a monument (to them)." The mention of those by whom the monument was erected is a very early characteristic, and points to a date in the fifth century—a period suggested also by the only slightly debased and unligatured character of the lettering. (See additional Note, p. 102.)

Fig. 50. A cross-marked slab, in blue slate, 2 feet 1½ inches high, from Elachnave, now in the National Museum of Antiquities. For another similar cross in the old burial ground at Elachnave, see *ECM,* part III, p. 403, Fig. 421.

Fig. 51. The mutilated fragment of a fine sculptured free-standing cross of early date in St. Columba's churchyard, Canna. The cross is in yellow sandstone, and in its present state is 7 feet high. For a description of the subjects carved on it see *ECM,* part III., pp. 107-9. According to *Stuart,* Vol. II., Notices of the Plates, p. 29, the beast (now almost indistinguishable) on the remaining arm of the cross was a *camel.* A beast not unlike a camel seems to be depicted on one of the stones at Meigle (*ECM,* part III., Fig. 310B).

Fig. 52. A and B. Front and back views of a sculptured slab, perhaps the fragment of a cross shaft, also from Canna. The fragment measures 2 feet long.

Fig. 53. A and B. Front and back views of a fine sculptured slab of Class II., which was found in removing the walls of the old parish church (St. Colmoc's) of Kirriemuir. The slab is in sandstone, and is 1 foot 11 inches high. On the front is a cross with interlaced work, dividing the panel into four compartments. In the upper two compartments are human figures with eagle heads, while below are two ecclesiastics each holding a book. The back of the slab is divided into two pictures, the upper one apparently showing St. Paul and St. Anthony sharing bread in the desert, while the lower shows a seated figure, with the "mirror" and "comb" symbols on the left hand side and an unknown symbol on the right.

Fig. 54. A and B. This notable monument of Class II also was discovered in the foundations of the old parish church of Kirriemuir. It is in yellow sandstone, and is 2 feet 9 inches high. On the front is a fine enriched cross; at either side of its head two angels kneel in adoration; while on the left of the shaft is a man with cloak and staff, and on the right a bird of prey seizing a stag, below which are a nondescript animal and two galloping hounds. The back of the slab contains a single panel, on the upper part of which is a mounted warrior, while below a horseman with his hound pursues a fleeing stag, whose hind leg the hound has already seized. Beside the upper horseman is the "double disc and Z-rod" symbol. As usual in Pictish sculpture, the scenes of action on this slab are wrought with great spirit.

Fig. 55. A, B and C. Front, back and right side views of a sculptured slab (Class III.) at Dunkeld Cathedral. It is in sandstone, and is 4 feet 10 inches high. This monument long served as a gatepost, and is thus sorely defaced. The upper part of the front shows an army of infantry and cavalry on the march, while below them is a group of three fallen, one headless. Underneath this scene is a crude representation of what seems to be intended for Daniel in the lions' den ; and at the foot of the slab, which is mutilated, are the heads of a row of men. On either side is a recessed panel, of which the right one displays a grotesque beast with a long snout and curling tail between his legs. The reverse of the slab is divided into three panels. On the upper part is a row of heads, probably representing a multitude, to the left of which may be dimly discerned a figure holding a large circular disc. This may be intended to represent the miracle of the loaves and fishes (but *cf.* Anderson, *Scotland in Early Christian Times,* Second Series, p. 157). Below this scene are two rows of figures clad in long gowns. The right side of the stone shows a man on horseback on top, a large figure of a nimbed Saint, and three smaller figures below. The sculpturing on the left edge of the slab is almost destroyed, save an escaping spiral at the top (see *Stuart,* Vol. I., plates L. and LI.). The art of this stone is extremely debased.

For other stones at Dunkeld see *ECM*, part III., pp. 319, 342, and *Stuart,* Vol. II., plates XVI. and LXVIII. Dr. Stuart has a pertinent comment (Vol. II., Notices of the Plates, p. 10) : "it would seem that the impulse which gave rise to the numerous sculptured crosses with symbols which are found in early ecclesiastical sites in ancient Pictland, had declined before the era of the establishment of Dunkeld. The sculptured crosses which occur at St. Andrews—another Scottish [i.e., Scotic] foundation—are also destitute of the peculiar features of the monuments of Pictland."

Fig. 56. Sculptured stone in the King's Park, Dunkeld. This is a recumbent slab of grey sandstone, 3 feet 6 inches long, incised with the representation of a mounted lancer blowing a horn.

Fig. 57. One of two sculptured monuments of Celto-Anglian type found at Inchcolm. This sandstone slab is 2 feet 2½ inches high. The second stone is a hog-backed monument, and is illustrated in *ECM,* part III., p. 366, Fig. 385. In the sixteenth century there still existed other monuments seemingly of Celtic type at Inchcolm, as appears from a passage in Bellenden's *Boece,* Vol. II., p. 258. The Danes, he tells us, having been defeated by Macbeth and Banquo, "gaif gret sowmes of gold to Makbeth to suffer thair friendis that war slane at his jeoperd to be buryit in Sanct Colmes Inche. In memory heirof, mony auld sepulturis ar yit in the said Inche, gravin with armis of Danis."

Fig. 58. A and B. External and interior views of the oratory on Inchcolm. This interesting little structure has been fully described by Sir James Y. Simpson (*Proc. Soc. Ant. Scot.,* Vol. II., pp. 489-528). It measures about

16 feet in internal length, and 6 feet 3 inches in greatest breadth.   The general style of the building is purely Celtic, but the vaulted roof with its grouted and flagged covering, and the arched doorway, indicate continental influence.   Thus the *mos Scotorum* and the *mos Romanorum* are found in interpenetration in the same building.

Fig. 59.   A and B.   Front and back views of a remarkable cross slab from Kilmorie Chapel, Kirkcolm.   The stone is a slab of greywacke, 5 feet 4 inches high.   On the front the sculpturing is incised, and shows a Crucifixion—the Saviour's legs, after the Irish fashion, not being crossed. Below is the figure of a man, with his hands clasped in front, as if in prayer.   On his right side are two birds apparently pecking at him, and on his left a pair of pincers, above which are two indeterminate objects. These may be intended for playing counters, the dice and the pincers being symbols of the Passion.   The reverse of the monument shows an equal-armed cross highly enriched with foliaceous scroll-work, and resting on a pedestal, which is carved with a design composed of (1) two horn-like objects with what seems a grotesque lacertine creature between them : (2) a serpent whose body forms a mass of convoluted ornament ; and (3) two more serpents with their bodies interwined in complicated knotwork.   The sculpture on this side of the stone is in bold relief.   The presence of foliaged ornament on the cross speaks for a late period, and the design bears evidences of debasement : yet it is so superior in technique to the incredible crudeness of the Crucifixion on the other side as to suggest that the stone has been turned about and the Crucifixion added at a later date.

Fig. 60.   A recumbent slab with incised cross of loose plaitwork, from the *Releig Orain,* Iona.   This slab is of sandstone (not native to the island), and measures 4 feet 5 inches long.   It will be noted that the plaitwork of the cross is combined with a square ring (*cf.* note to Fig. 43).   The general resemblance of the cross to the Hartlepool-Lindisfarne and Clonmacnoise groups of crosses (Fig. 39-42) will be at once apparent : and it is evident that this cross at Iona supplies a valuable connecting link between the Irish and the Northumbrian groups, affording an archæological commentary on the historical connection, *viâ* Iona, between the Irish Church and the Church of the Angles.

For another cross slab of the same design at Iona see *ECM,* part III., p. 390, Fig. 405.

Fig. 61.   A recumbent cross-slab of mica schist, 3 feet 9 inches long, from the Nunnery at Iona.   The form of the cross and the design of its interlaced enrichment indicate a later date than the monument previously described.

Fig. 62.   A and B.   Front and back views of St. Martin's Cross, Iona. Now, at all events, this is pre-eminently the High Cross of St. Columba's

N

sacred isle, and it is significant that it should bear the venerated name of
the founder of Celtic monasticism. The cross is in red granite, and measures
16 feet 8 inches high, including the pedestal. The front bears, as the principal
feature in its decorative and devotional composition, what has been a very
dignified representation of the Virgin Mother and Child in Glory, surrounded
by adoring angels. This design occupies a large circular plaque in the centre
of the cross : on the arms at either side are rampant beasts, and three pairs
of grotesque beasts devouring their interlocked tails occupy the head of the
cross. The designs on the shaft are apparently scenes from Holy Writ, of
which Daniel in the lions' den (*cf.* Fig. 55) and David playing before Saul,
are still recognisable.   At the base of the carving is a swirled design of
serpents and bosses of plaitwork. The back of the cross is sculptured with
panels composed of bosses of plaitwork, spirals, grotesque beasts, and
serpents. The base and the edges of the cross are plain, but the faces of the
ring are decorated with interlaced work. This noble cross is purely Irish in
all its features, and dates probably from the tenth century.

Fig. 63.   A—D. The Camuston Cross, now in the grounds of Panmure
House, Forfarshire. It is in sandstone, and is 6 feet 6 inches high. On the
front a Crucifixion—with Longinus piercing Our Lord's side and Stephaton
proffering the sponge with vinegar—occupies the whole head of the cross ;
while the shaft is divided into two panels, the upper one showing a centaur
with bow and arrow, and the lower one a scrolled foliaceous design.   The
back of the cross is similarly arranged, the main design (corresponding to
the Crucifixion in front) being Christ now risen in Glory, saluted by adoring
angels, while below are the four evangelists in pairs, each with his Gospel.
This free-standing cross, displaying a Crucifixion, is of Irish not Pictish
type ; and its clumsy design and debased carving are signs of the late and
decadent period at which this form of monument began, under the Scotic
domination of the Alpin dynasty, to intrude itself into Pictland.   The
balancing of Christ Crucified and Christ in Glory is a very Irish motive, as
is also the roof-like apex of the Cross.

Fig. 64.   A and B. The Kildalton Cross, front and back views. It is
in red sandstone, and is 9 feet high. In a short note it is futile to attempt
any description, much less interpretation, of this bewilderingly elaborate and
most beautiful High Cross, which dates probably from the tenth century.
It has been fully discussed, and its symbolism and ornament analysed in
masterly fashion, by Dr. Joseph Anderson in a note furnished to R. C.
Graham's *The Carved Stones of Islay,* from which work these photographs
are reproduced.   The cross stands on its original site in the churchyard of
St. John the Evangelist at Kildalton. While the general design of the cross
associates it completely with St. Martin's Cross at Iona (Fig. 62) and with the
Irish High Crosses of the same period, it is noteworthy that the Kildalton
Cross differs from St. Martin's Cross in certain features pointing perhaps to
Pictish influence—such as the absence of a Crucifixion on one side, balanced

by a Christ in Glory on the other (as in the Camuston Cross, Fig. 63); and also the predominance of ornament over figure subjects. The figure subjects represented include the Virgin and Child in Glory, occupying quite a subordinate position on the front of the shaft; David rending the lion's jaws; and the sacrifice of Isaac. The whirligig patterns of serpents and bosses connect the Kildalton Cross with St. Martin's Cross, which it resembles also in the plainness of its base.

Fig. 65. A and B. Front and back views of the High Cross of Prior Colin at Oronsay Priory. (He died in 1510.) This splendid monument illustrates the peculiar form into which the great free-standing and glorified High Crosses of the West Coast developed towards the close of the period of Celtic art in the later Middle Ages. The nimbus or glory encircling the cross has now become a solid disc, from which the head and arms project. The Crucifixion is of ordinary medieval type, with the Saviour's feet nailed : it is in a very fine style of art. Alongside interlaced ornament, preserving the old Celtic tradition, is seen the later conventional scrolled foliaceous enrichment. At the base of the shaft on both sides this scroll work runs off from the tails of two grotesque animals quite in the old style. The cross is 12 feet high, excluding the pedestal.

Fig. 66. An early Christian inscribed stone at Kirkmadrine, upper part. It is a rough unshaped schistose monolith, 7 feet high, upon which is incised the encircled Chi-Rho monogram (made with a Roman R, *cf.* note to Fig. 48), and below it the imperfect inscription, in debased Roman capitals :—

> ......S ET
> FLOREN
> TIVS

Fig. 67. Early Christian stone at Whithorn. This is an unshaped pillar stone, 4 feet high, incised with the Chi-Rho monogram, which here assumes the unique form of a segmented and wheeled cross on a pedestal. The R is again of Roman type. Underneath are incised, in very debased Roman capitals, the words :—

> LOC STI
> PETRI APV
> STOLI

"The place of St. Peter the Apostle." The form of the first S betrays Celtic influence. This monument is clearly somewhat later than the two Kirkmadrine Stones (Figs. 48 and 66) and probably belongs to the sixth century. It was probably a termon or girth cross, marking the boundaries of the monastic lands.

Fig. 68. A free-standing cross of later date (probably tenth century) at Whithorn, showing the form derived from the Chi-Rho monogram on the earliest Christian stones. This cross is in green slate, and measures 4 feet 10 inches high. The type of cross thus developed became characteristic of the Britonic Kingdom of Strathclyde (see p. 76, note 3).

Fig. 69. Incised stone at Arbirlot, near Arbroath, Forfarshire. It is an unshaped monolith of whinstone, 5 feet 6 inches high, upon which are carved two equal-armed crosses, and two objects that look like open books, the lower apparently furnished with a clasp. Beside the upper book is a circle, possibly meant to indicate the Host. The cross at the base of the stone and the upper book are connected by a curious incised channel.

Arbirlot was the site of an ancient Celtic monastery, under the patronage of St. Ninian, who in all probability was its founder. Between 1201 and 1207 charters in the *Registrum Vetus de Aberbrothock* (pp. 29-32) are witnessed by Maurice, Abbot of Abireloth: and thus we learn that the Celtic monastery preserved its identity until the beginning of the thirteenth century. For the group of Ninianic sites in the neighbourhood of Arbroath see Scott, *Pictish Nation,* pp. 83-4.

Fig. 70. St. Mochriecha's Cross, Balnagowan Wood, Aboyne. An equal-armed cross incised on a boulder 3 feet high. See my *Origins of Christianity in Aberdeenshire,* pp. 17, 18.

Fig. 71. Incised equal-armed and wheeled cross, $8\frac{1}{2}$ inches in diameter, now preserved in the pavement of the west tower porch of the Norman church at Monymusk.

Fig. 72. Incised cross-slab at St. Fumoc's Church, Botriphnie, Banff-shire. See my paper in *Proc. Soc. Ant. Scot.,* Vol. LX., pp. 278-9. The over-all diameter of the cross is about 8 inches, and the length of the shaft is $5\frac{1}{4}$ inches. It will at once be apparent that this cross is a "skeletonised" form of the *Candida Casa* type shown in Fig. 67.

Fig. 73. A and B. Front and back views of the Bressay Stone (Class III.). This was found near the ruins of St. Mary's Church, Culbinsburgh, Isle of Bressay, Shetland. In addition to the sculpturings on the front and back, shown in our illustrations, there is an ogham inscription, in mixed Scandinavian and Celtic language, along both sides of the stone, which bears internal evidence of dating from the ninth century. A considerable amount of literature has grown up round this stone, and it would be out of place here to discuss the many intricate questions that it raises: reference may be made to the account in *ECM,* Part III., pp. 5-10, with authorities cited. For our present purpose the point of importance is the cross on the obverse. It is an equal-armed cross within a circle, the arms being expanded, and the spaces between them filled with interlaced work. The descent of this form of cross from the cross at Whithorn (Fig. 67) is quite obvious. On the reverse of the stone the cross is of a similar type. The two clerics below the cross on the front are carrying *bachuills* like that of St. Moluag (Fig. 36). The stone is a slab of chlorite schist 3 feet 9 inches high. It is now preserved in the National Museum of Antiquities at Edinburgh.

Fig. 74.   The Monymusk Stone (Class II.—see note to Fig. 31, *supra*). Now preserved at Monymusk House, this stone originally stood at Nether Mains, about a mile eastward.   It is an unhewn striated granitic boulder, 7 feet high, displaying sculpture partly incised and partly in relief.   The sculpture consists of an equal-armed Celtic cross, with shaft and base, all ornamented with knotwork; the "step" symbol; and the "disc and double-ring" symbol—both symbols being enriched.   In *Proc. Soc. Ant. Scot.,* Vol. LIX., pp. 36-9, I have exhaustively discussed this remarkable monument, and adduced reasons for attributing it to the ninth century.   Since then I have come across a piece of evidence from Ireland, pointing in the same direction.   It is the tombstone of St. Berechtuir of Tullylease, who died in 839.   This stone bears an equal-armed cross on a shaft which is structurally separate, exactly similar in design to the cross at Monymusk.   See the illustration in Champneys, *Irish Ecclesiastical Architecture,* Plate XXVIII., and p. 77.   (See also note to Fig. 31.)

Fig. 75.   The Papil Stone (Class III.).   An upright slab of red sandstone, 6 feet 10 inches high, found prostrate near the old church of Papil, West Burra, Shetland, and now preserved in the National Museum of Antiquities, Edinburgh.   The kinship of the cross on this stone with that on the Bressay Stone (Fig. 73) will at once be recognised, and the resemblance of both to the Strathclyde crosses (Figs. 67 and 68) is equally obvious.   Such resemblances clearly point to *Candida Casa* of St. Ninian as the ultimate source from which the equal-armed and wheeled slab-crosses of eastern Pictland were derived. The figures of ecclesiastics below the cross are very interesting, and closely resemble those on the Bressay Stone, like them carrying curved *bachuills* (*cf.* Fig. 36) and book-satchels.   The beast below these figures is a notable example of Pictish skill in animal portraiture (see p. 78).   What is signified by the two bird-monsters pecking at a human head is quite unknown.   See the very full discussion of this interesting stone in *ECM,* part III., pp. 10-15.

Fig. 76.   High Cross at the roofless church of St. Charmaig (Cormac) at Keills, Knapdale.   This fine cross in blue slate measures 7 feet 4 inches high, and with its tall head and stunted arms belongs to a purely Irish type of the tenth century.   The ornament consists of a mass of very bold figure sculpture grouped round an enriched central boss, while on the shaft are found (1) a panel of fretwork; (2) a panel of interlaced work, with four beasts whose tails are involved in the pattern; and (3) a basal design of escaping spiral work.   The figure sculpture is extremely vigorous.   On the head of the cross is an angel treading a serpent underfoot, while the arms and the top of the shaft are occupied by a spirited representation of Daniel in the lions' den.   The back of the cross is plain.

For Keills church and its sculptured slabs see W. C. Crawford in *Proc. Soc. Ant. Scot.,* Vol. LIV, pp. 248-52.

Fig. 77. Incised symbol stone of Class I., formerly at Newbigging Leslie, Insch, Aberdeenshire, but now removed to Leith Hall. This stone is illustrated as an example of Pictish skill in animal portraiture (see p. 78). It is a slab of red Bennachie granite, about 2 feet 1 inch by 1 foot 3 inches, upon which are carved the "rectangle" symbol, and the "mirror" and "comb" symbols, all enriched : also the figure of a wolf, which is drawn with consummate artistry and perfect fidelity to nature.

Dr. Joseph Anderson (*Scotland in Early Christian Times,* Second Series, p. 170), sought to find in this stone a representation of the symbolic "tigress gazing into the mirror" of the medieval Bestiaries. But the fact that the mirror occurs on this stone in association with the comb, as on so many other Pictish monuments where a "tigress" is not in question, seems decisive against this supposition.

Fig. 78. Another and most striking example of superb Pictish animal portraiture. This is a red granite slab, 4 feet high, in the churchyard of Inverurie. On it is incised an extremely spirited and masterly drawing of a prancing horse. The skill with which the sculptors (or should we hazard "sculptor"?) of this and the Newbigging Leslie stone have wrought in the obdurate granite, is altogether remarkable.

Additional Note to Fig. 49.

The foregoing matter was already in paged proof before the appearance of the November, 1926, number of *Scottish Gaelic Studies* (Vol. I., part 2). In it at p. 200, Mr. F. C. Diack comments on the "bad Latin" of the accepted reading of the *Latinus* stone, and propounds a new explanation of his own. He proposes to read the seventh line as one word, ANNIV, which he regards as a woman's name, and so translates the inscription as follows :—"We praise thee Lord. Latinus aged 35 years and his daughter Anniu. Here the descendants of Barrovados made this monument."

I must confess that this suggested new reading seems to me singularly unconvincing. Surely the merest glance at the spacing of the letters in line seven will show that it consists of two words, ANNI V, and not ANNIV. The accepted rendering seems also in harmony with the whole epigraphic balance of the legend. Certainly the Latinity leaves something to be desired, but this is quite on a level with the debased character of the script, and is in entire accordance with what we should expect in the general circumstances of an outlying and partly Romanised Celtic congregation.

Fig. 1

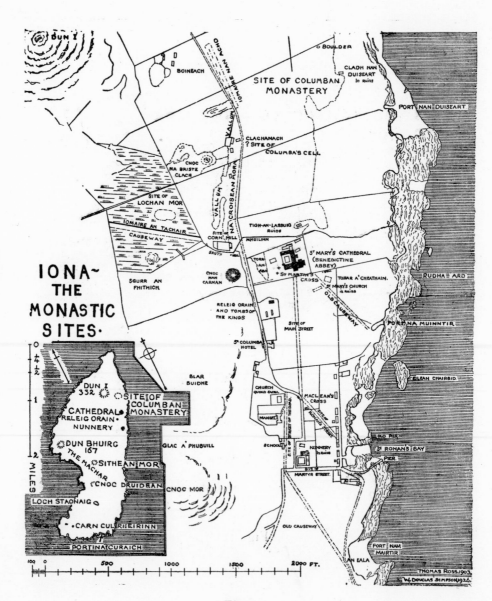

Fig. 2

Fig. 3

Fig. 4

Fig. 5

Fig. 6

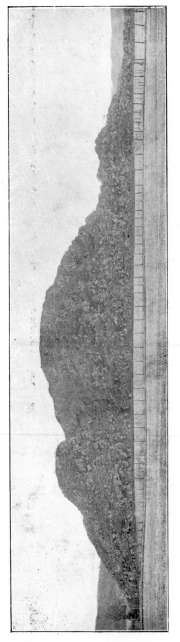

Fig. 7 A

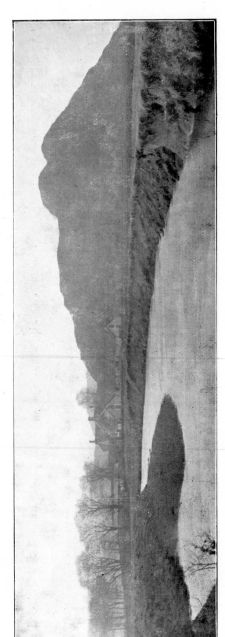

Fig. 7 B

Fig. 8

Fig. 9

Fig. 10

Fig. 11

Fig. 12

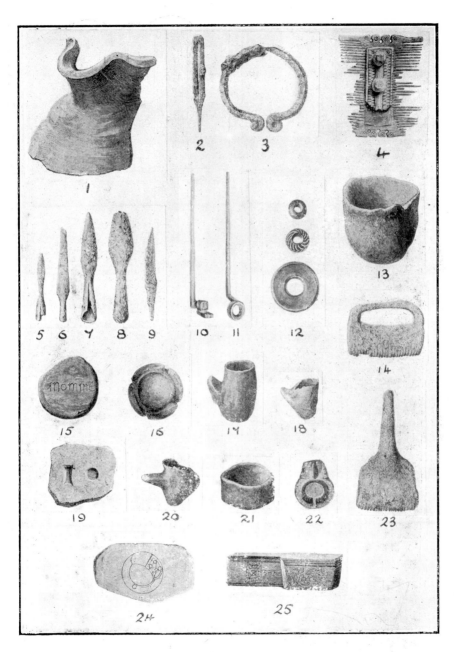

Fig. 13

Fig. 14 A   Fig. 14 B

Fig. 15

Fig. 16

Fig. 17

Fig. 18

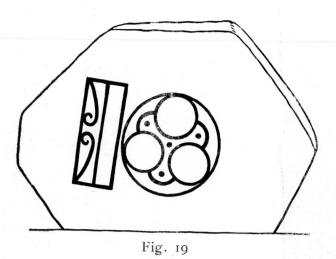

Fig. 19

Fig. 20

Fig. 21

Fig. 22 A   Fig. 22 B

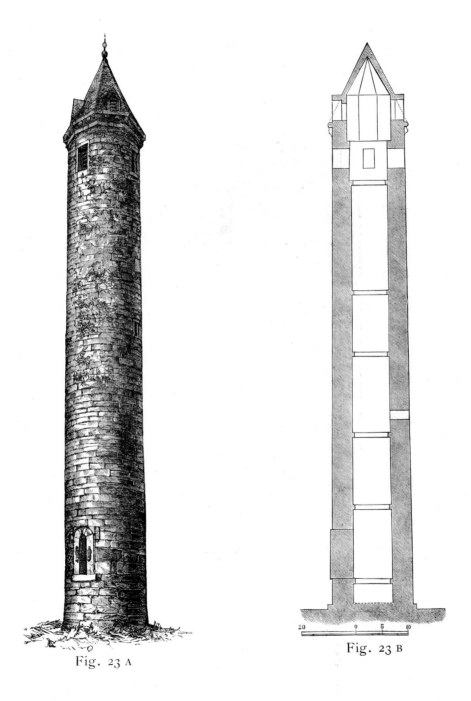

Fig. 23 A

Fig. 23 B

Fig. 24

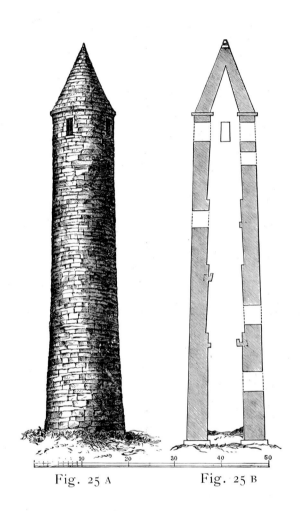

Fig. 25 A   Fig. 25 B

CULDEE STATIONS
IN SCOTLAND.
W. Douglas Simpson, 1924.

DORNOCH
ROSEMARKY
MONYMUSK.
BRECHIN.
DUNKELD
MONIFIETH
ABERNETHY
LISMORE
KILRYMONT
(St Andrews)
MUTHILL.
IONA
DUNBLANE.
LOCHLEVEN.

Fig. 26

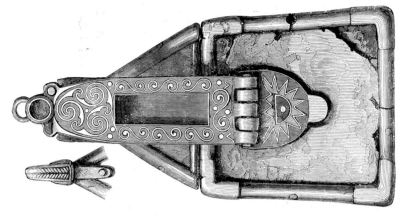

Fig. 27 B

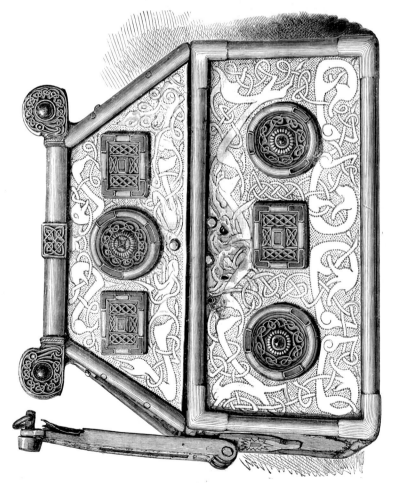

Fig. 27 A

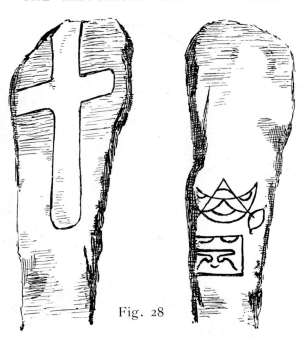

Fig. 28

Fig. 29

Fig. 30

Fig. 31

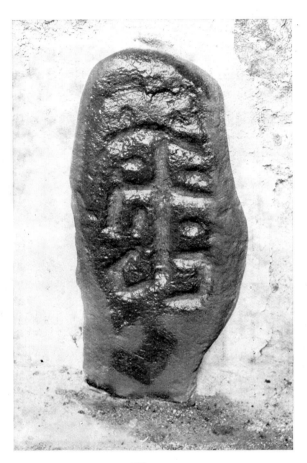

Fig. 32

Fig. 33

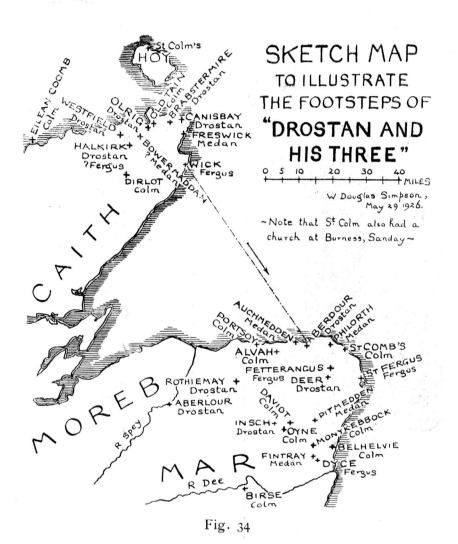

SKETCH MAP
TO ILLUSTRATE
THE FOOTSTEPS OF
"DROSTAN AND
HIS THREE"

0 5 10   20   30   40
├──┼──┼────┼────┼────┼────┤ MILES

W. Douglas Simpson,
May 29 1926.

~Note that St Colm also had a
church at Burness, Sanday ~

Fig. 34

R

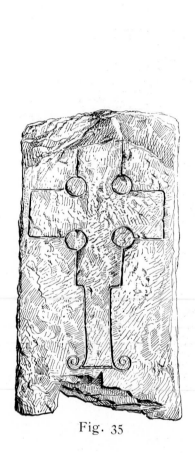

Fig. 35

Fig. 36

Fig. 37

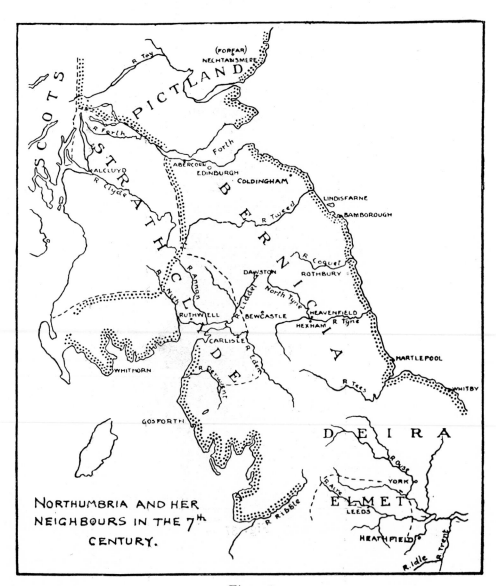

Fig. 38

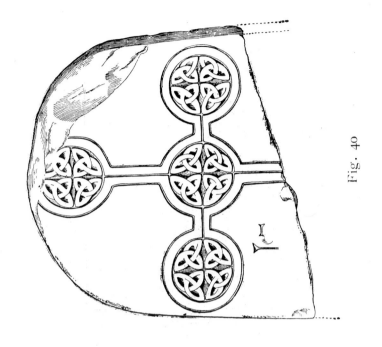

Fig. 40

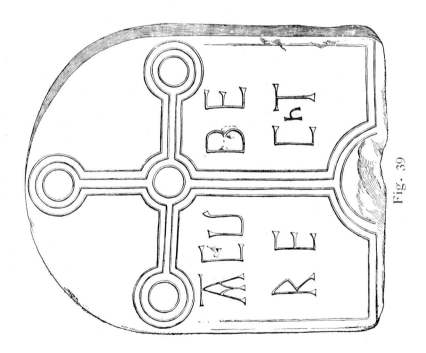

Fig. 39

Fig. 41

Fig. 42

Fig. 43

Fig. 44 A

Fig. 44 B

Fig. 45 A   Fig. 45 B

Fig. 46 A   Fig. 46 B   Fig. 46 C   Fig. 46 D

Fig. 47 A

Fig. 47 B

Fig. 47 C   Fig. 47 D

Fig. 48

Fig. 49

Fig. 51

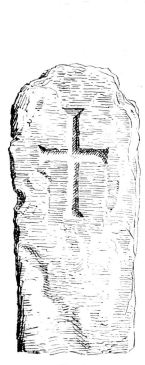

Fig. 50

T

Fig. 52 A   Fig. 52 B

Fig. 53 B

Fig. 53 A

Fig. 54 A

Fig. 54 B

Fig. 55 C

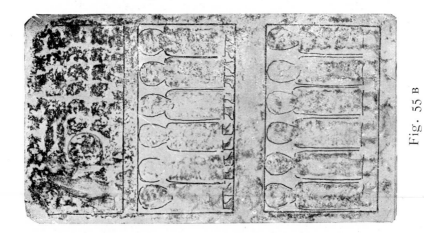

Fig. 55 B

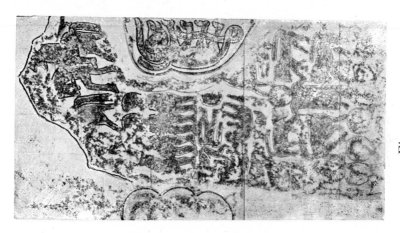

Fig. 55 A

Fig. 56

Fig. 57

Fig. 58 A

Fig. 58 B

Fig. 59 A

U

Fig. 59 B

Fig. 60

Fig. 61

Fig. 62 A

Fig. 62 B

Fig. 63 A   Fig. 63 B

Fig. 63 C   Fig. 63 D

Fig. 64 A

Fig. 64 B

X

Fig. 65 A

Fig. 65 B

Fig. 66

Fig. 67

Fig. 68

Fig. 69

Fig. 70

Fig. 71

Fig. 72

Fig. 73 A

Fig. 73 B

Fig. 74

Fig. 75

Fig. 76

Fig. 77

Fig. 78

INDEX.

Z